The BREAD MACHINE Gourmet

SHEA MACKENZIE

Avery Publishing Group
Garden City Park, New York

Cover designer: William Gonzalez

Cover photographer: John Strange

Interior color photographs: John Strange

Editor: Rick Mastelli

Book designer: Deborah Fillion

Publisher's Cataloging in Publication
(Prepared by Quality Books Inc.)

MacKenzie, Shea, 1945–
   The bread machine gourmet : simple recipes for extraordinary
breads / Shea MacKenzie.
   p. cm.
   Includes index
   ISBN 0-89529-697-7

   1. Bread. 2. Automatic bread machines. I. Title.

TX769.M54 1993   641.8'15
                                  QBI93-977

Printed in the United States of America

19   18   17   16   15   14   13   12   11

$\mathcal{C}$ONTENTS

PREFACE

As our daily lives become more and more complicated and our environment more hazardous, how we live and what we eat takes on greater and greater significance. Living today requires not only stamina and energy but a sense of responsibility for our personal welfare and the welfare of those we love. We need and want to exercise more control in our lives. One thing we can do is to return to a healthier pattern of eating.

Since the advent of civilization, bread has been a cornerstone of our diets. Coarse, hearty, fiber-filled loaves of nutritious bread were essential to the lives of our ancestors. Bread has been made and enjoyed daily for centuries. By the 1950s, however, with the advent of fast foods and factory-made baked goods, uniform loaves of sandwich bread with doughy white interiors began to replace what we once called our staff of life. While marvelous for making spitballs to shoot across the classroom, these loaves bear no resem-

blance to the home-baked bread of our past; they have little taste and even less nutritional value.

Fortunately, I missed this white-bread revolution by growing up in Europe, where I feasted on long, thin, crusty loaves of French bread; light, flaky croissants; and rich, buttery, shiny brioche. These breads were made lovingly by hand and created without preservatives. Each small neighborhood in the city in which I lived had at least one corner bakery filled with enticing sights and aromas. By early dawn, the tantalizing scent of freshly baked bread drifted through the streets, and each morning would find those same streets crowded with housewives carrying that day's bread home in string bags. It was not until I returned to the United States that I was confronted with factory-produced white bread, and bread became a less important part of my diet.

Many years later, I began to bake my own breads in an attempt to recapture the wonderful tastes and textures of my childhood. I became enamored not only with the delicious breads I created but also with the satisfaction I found when working dough. Today, more and more cooks are discovering this sense of fulfillment. They are enjoying a renewed appreciation of the hearty, whole grain, and nutritionally rich foods of our heritage. They are rediscovering the nutritional impact that is locked in each kernel of grain. Armed with this information, they have begun to return whole-grain breadmaking to its rightful place as a vital, necessary, and delicious component of a healthy diet.

The Bread Machine Gourmet focuses on returning bread to its natural, wholesome goodness using methods that are consistent with our modern lives and times. Filled with a wide variety of recipes, this book is designed to help you create breads ranging from simple, basic loaves to more intricate creations that incorporate fruit, nuts, vegetables, or grains. Most of the recipes use an automatic breadmaker for the complete mixing, kneading, rising, and baking of the loaves. There are many recipes, however, that use the machine only for mixing and kneading, allowing you to form the dough by hand into special loaves, rolls, or bread sticks.

The Bread Machine Gourmet introduces you to the fascinating world of whole-grain breadmaking using an automatic bread machine. I hope that it inspires you and helps you discover the nutritional goodness and the fabulous tastes and aromas of your own fresh-baked breads.

WELCOME TO AUTOMATIC BREADMAKING

A phenomenon is sweeping the country, one that is destined to put behind us forever the tedious and time-consuming bread-making methods of our grandmothers. Over the years, laborsaving inventions from toasters to food processors have moved into American kitchens, facilitating food preparation and improving our time in the kitchen and its results. In recent years, however, the usefulness of these new devices has become marginal, and we have suffered instead an assault of unnecessary gadgets. It has been many years since a useful, truly innovative labor-saving device has been introduced. And many years, too, have passed since a kitchen tool has generated any excitement.

Why a need for automatic breadmaking? Traditional breadmaking has always been a labor-intensive process,

calling for physical stamina and undivided attention. A single loaf of bread requires careful measuring and mixing of ingredients, time-consuming kneading, and constant attention to ensure proper rising and baking. With each bread-making attempt, uncertainties abound: Have I kneaded enough? Is the dough elastic enough? Is there too much flour? Has the dough risen properly? And so on.

Our home kitchens and our busy, complicated lives are not well suited to the traditional methods of breadmaking. Baking with yeast requires more attention, time, and patience than most of us have on a daily basis. While we are once again using natural ingredients in our meals, we are not willing to revert to old-fashioned cooking methods, no matter how satisfying. Simply put, no one has time anymore. Our lives and our kitchens have been waiting for a simpler way to make one of our staple foods: bread.

Automatic breadmakers, in their many forms and sizes, are rapidly becoming an essential part of the good cook's kitchen. They are revolutionizing how the home baker makes bread. Having hot, crusty, nutritious bread at any time of day is simply not a lot of work anymore.

About Automatic Breadmakers

An automatic breadmaker is simple to operate and requires very little effort on your part. You have only to measure the ingredients, place them in the bread pan, and fit the pan inside the machine. To program the unit for the proper bread mode, simply press the appropriate button. That's it!

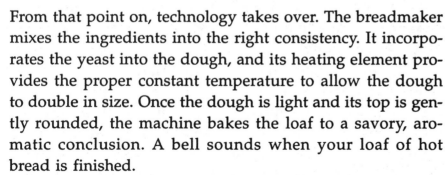

From that point on, technology takes over. The breadmaker mixes the ingredients into the right consistency. It incorporates the yeast into the dough, and its heating element provides the proper constant temperature to allow the dough to double in size. Once the dough is light and its top is gently rounded, the machine bakes the loaf to a savory, aromatic conclusion. A bell sounds when your loaf of hot bread is finished.

There are many different automatic breadmakers on the market today. While all have some common characteristics, each offers a slightly different approach or capacity. All of the units are squarish in shape and weigh 14 to 20 pounds. They're designed to sit on your kitchen counter and use 120-volt household current. A programming device is built into the machine, so you can select the method and baking time. Many machines have a small yeast dispenser on the top of the unit, while others instruct you to add the yeast directly to the ingredients in the bread pan. I have tried both methods and have seen no difference in the final result. Each unit has a bread pan with a handle and a kneading blade that fits inside metal guides in the cavity of the machine. All machines provide an instruction pamphlet with a few sample recipes.

The differences between the machines can be significant. Capacity should be addressed first. Most breadmakers produce 1- or 1^1/2-pound loaves. The 1-pound loaf is about 7 inches long and approximately 5 inches in diameter; it yields 8 or 9 fairly thick slices of bread. The 1^1/2-pound loaf is 8 to 9 inches long and about 6^1/2 inches in diameter. It

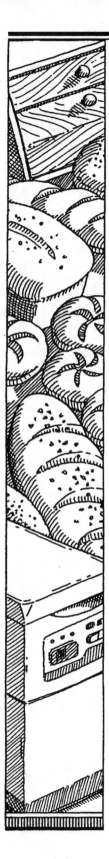

yields about 12 slices. When considering the various bread-makers, size can be an important factor, especially if you have a large family.

The types of flour you intend to use should be another consideration when selecting a bread machine. If you are a whole-grain baker, a machine with a separate cycle for these breads is a better choice. These units provide a longer rising time to accommodate the heavier, coarser flour. While this is not necessary, the loaves will be lighter if they are allowed to rise an extra hour.

Another factor to consider when selecting a bread-maker is its cooling cycle. Some machines circulate cool air around the baked loaf for 30 minutes, which allows the bread to cool and the steam to escape. When this is not done and the baked bread remains in the closed unit, the steam penetrates the loaf, causing it to slice unevenly or become sticky. If your machine does not have a cooling cycle, it is best to plan on removing the bread immediately after baking.

The selection of baking modes varies with each machine, but most breadmakers have a standard cycle for white-flour breads and a longer cycle for whole wheat loaves. In addition, some machines have a *light-bake* mode, which creates a loaf of white bread with a light-colored crust. Other models offer options for light, medium, and dark crusts.

Some machines have a *rapid-bake* cycle in either the standard or whole-grain mode. When this cycle is used, the ingredients are mixed and the dough is kneaded and allowed to rise as normal, but the loaf is baked faster than

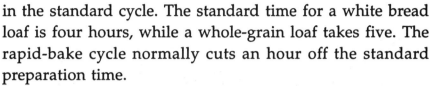

in the standard cycle. The standard time for a white bread loaf is four hours, while a whole-grain loaf takes five. The rapid-bake cycle normally cuts an hour off the standard preparation time.

Machines with a *dough mode* are truly versatile. They mix and knead the dough, then allow it to rise. Once the dough has risen, you can remove it to form it into pizza crusts, rolls, long thin loaves of French bread, bagels, or even pita pockets, which you then can bake in your conventional oven. The dough mode thus assumes the most laborious and time-consuming steps of breadmaking.

Most breadmakers have timers, which allow you to combine the ingredients and program the machine to start at a later time. This option lets you wake up to the smell of freshly baked bread. A note of caution: When using the timer, bake only a bread with ingredients that will not spoil when left sitting at room temperature.

Using an automatic breadmaker can be fun and exciting. But more than a new toy, a bread machine is a time- and laborsaving invention that gives us more quality time for our family, our friends, and ourselves.

CHAPTER 1

Getting Started

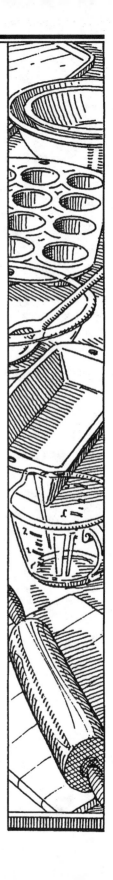

Baking good bread is not an exact science but rather a labor of love. And the more you love creating loaves of hot, wonderfully textured bread, the more skilled you will become. Breads, partly because they're composed of so few ingredients, offer terrific opportunities for experimentation, and are forgiving of mistakes. An automatic breadmaker makes the process all the more easy and accessible, since the machine does most of the work. There are, however, a number of factors that will contribute to the success of your loaf. What follows is a list of guidelines to help you find consistent success with your home-baked breads.

Ingredient temperature. Even though the machine may have a "rest" cycle, which allows the ingredients to be gently warmed before mixing, it is best to start with ingredients that are room temperature.

Room temperature. High humidity or extreme cold can affect your finished bread. For best results, reserve breadmaking for those days when the room temperature is between 67° and 77°F.

Measurements. Most breads that fail do so because of careless measuring. When baking bread by hand, experience will tell you if you need more liquid or flour. In a bread machine, however, there is no opportunity to "feel" your dough. You must rely on your recipe and the accurate measurement of ingredients. Proper utensils are important for precise measuring.

When measuring dry ingredients, use a measuring cup designed for this purpose. Scoop the dry ingredient into the cup and gently mound it over the rim. Do not tap the bottom of the cup or do anything else that might settle the ingredients. Use the flat side of a knife or spatula to level the top. Liquid ingredients should be measured in a liquid measuring cup.

You may notice that in recipes using whole-grain flour, more flour is called for than in recipes using only bread flour. The reason is that breads made with whole grains are denser and do not rise as much as those made with white flour. I also add more yeast in whole-grain recipes for the same reason.

For more information on measuring cups and utensils, see Breadmaking Utensils beginning on page 10.

Freshness of ingredients. If your loaf of bread comes out heavy and leaden, you probably used ingredients that were past their prime. Yeast is a notorious culprit, yet any of the other ingredients on the following list can also contribute to a bread's failure:

• *Yeast.* There are two forms of active yeast: compressed cake and dry granulated. All the yeast-bread recipes in this book call for the dry granulated type, as it is the one most readily available. It comes in $1/4$-ounce packages, with almost 3 teaspoons in a package. Once the package has been opened, the remaining yeast will keep for about one week in the refrigerator.

Yeast ferments when it is mixed with flour and liquid, converting starch to carbon dioxide. The gluten in flour captures the gas and stretches, causing the dough to rise. Depending on the recipe, the dough will rise once or twice before it is baked, with the yeast fermenting one last time before dying.

When buying yeast, it is difficult to determine freshness with any certainty. The expiration date on the package is a fairly reliable indicator of age, but it cannot tell you whether the yeast was subjected to extreme temperatures during transport or storage. This is why it is important to check, or *proof*, the yeast before using it to ascertain its freshness. Proofing yeast is easy. Simply fill a cup with warm water (110° to 115°F) and add a little yeast. If the yeast is fresh, the water will turn foamy within 5 minutes. If the water does not foam, the yeast is past its prime; it will not cause the bread to rise and should be discarded.

When dissolving yeast, be sure the water is neither too hot nor too cold. If the water is over 120°F, it will kill the yeast. On the other hand, if the water is too cold, the yeast will work too slowly. Cake yeast, which is more perishable than the active dry type, will stay up to 2 weeks in the refrigerator or 2 months in the freezer. Active dry yeast (even in unopened packages) should be stored in the refrigerator, where it will keep for several months.

• *Eggs.* While eggs should be used at room temperature, they should be kept refrigerated until 20 minutes before they are used. Eggs should be very fresh.

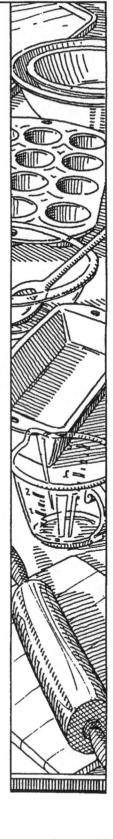

• *Flours.* Whole wheat flour, unlike white flour, is very perishable and must be fresh to make good bread. Each package should have a "pull" date. Avoid flour that has been on the shelf for more than 2 months.

All flour should be placed in airtight containers to keep it fresh and insect-free. If you have the space, refrigerate or freeze the flour. In areas of the country where weevils are a problem, freezing flour for at least a week before opening the package will kill any larva that might be present. Allow the flour to come to room temperature before using it.

Timing. While the breadmaker assumes most of the timing responsibility, you must still pay attention. Many models allow you to add all the ingredients to the bread pan simultaneously, but I have found that certain liquid-absorbing ingredients, such as dried fruit, alter the consistency of the bread by absorbing the liquid prematurely. I suggest eliminating this problem in two ways. First, when a recipe calls for an ingredient that needs to be reconstituted, do so before adding it to the bread pan. I have also found that adding a reconstituted ingredient after the mixing has been completed (before the kneading cycle begins) works well. Most machines have a bell that sounds at the beginning of the knead cycle.

If your breadmaker does not have a "cool-down" cycle, you must promptly remove the finished loaf to prevent it from becoming sticky and difficult to slice.

Breadmaking Utensils

Whether you are making your bread by hand or are using an automatic breadmaker, proper measuring cups and spoons are essential for successful results. In addition, although an automatic bread-

maker eliminates the need for many conventional utensils used to make bread, certain recipes may require additional basic equipment. Here are the most commonly used breadmaking tools:

Dry measuring cups. These are plastic or metal cups that come in a basic set of four. The set includes measurements for $1/4$, $1/3$, $1/2$, and 1 cup.

Liquid measuring cup. Made of glass, metal, or plastic, a liquid measuring cup has a 1- to 4-cup capacity.

Measuring spoons. These plastic or metal spoons come in a basic set that includes measurements for $1/4$, $1/2$, and 1 teaspoon, as well as a measurement for 1 tablespoon.

Baking sheets. Also called cookie sheets, these versatile pans are rectangular in shape and come in a variety of sizes. Some have shallow sides, while others have no sides. It is useful to have a few baking sheets on hand.

Mixing bowls. These bowls, made of metal, glass, or plastic, come in a variety of sizes. They are useful for combining ingredients.

Cake pans. An 8- or 9-inch round or square metal or glass cake pan is useful for baking breads such as cinnamon or sticky buns.

Loaf pans. Loaf pans, which are made of glass or metal, vary slightly in size. The two most popular sizes are approximately 8x4x2 inches and 9x5x3 inches. A French bread pan resembles a pipe that has been cut in half horizontally; it is generally 15 to 18 inches long and is made of metal.

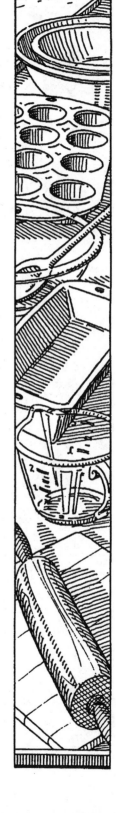

Muffin tins. The average muffin tin comes in stainless or tinned steel and has twelve 2-inch muffin cups. When using a muffin tin, it is important to fill any unused cups with water before placing in the oven. High oven heat can cause an empty cup to deform.

Saucepan. A small stainless steel, glass, or enamel saucepan is needed for breadmaking steps such as scalding milk.

Wire racks. These serve as cooling racks that allow air to circulate under the freshly baked loaves.

Rolling pin. A few of the recipes in this book suggest rolling out the dough before forming it into a loaf. Using your hands to pat out the dough is an acceptable substitute.

Food processor. While not a necessity, a food processor is nice to have for chopping, shredding, or grinding foods, seeds, or nuts.

Pot holders. Absolutely necessary for removing hot bread from either the oven or breadmaker.

Glossary of Ingredients

An unadorned loaf of bread is a very simple food, generally consisting of but a few ingredients. All yeast breads, no matter the taste, shape, or texture, begin with flour, water, and yeast. When you add additional ingredients to a basic bread recipe, you add character, dimension, and often more nutritional value. The following glossary describes the ingredients used in the recipes in this book. Keep in mind that the loaf of bread you create will be only as good and fresh as the ingredients that go into it.

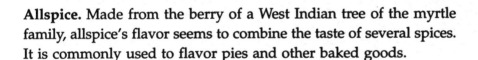

Allspice. Made from the berry of a West Indian tree of the myrtle family, allspice's flavor seems to combine the taste of several spices. It is commonly used to flavor pies and other baked goods.

Almonds. Slivered, toasted almonds add a nice crunch to breads but often do not have enough taste to add much in the way of flavor. I frequently suggest adding a dash of almond extract if the bread requires a pronounced almond flavor.

Amaretto. Derived mainly from apricot pits, amaretto is a syrupy sweet liqueur with a predominant flavor of bitter almonds. It is enhanced with the essences of vanilla, vanillin, and other flavorings. There are quite a few producers of amaretto today, but Italian producers dominate the market.

Anise. Clusters of tiny flowers and licorice-flavored seeds characterize the anise plant, which is native to the Mediterranean region. While the root of the anise is an herb that is used in some dishes, the seeds are more often used to flavor cakes, cookies, and liqueurs.

Asiago cheese. A wonderfully versatile Italian cheese, straw-colored Asiago is made from cow's milk. It has a nutty, sharp flavor and a semihard texture. Asiago is wonderful grated over pastas and delicious added to bread.

Basil. A sweet herb growing originally in India and tropical areas of Africa, basil was imported centuries ago into Mediterranean Europe, where it became a staple herb. Basil has a pleasant, pungent aroma. Its flavor enhances robust foods such as beans, pastas, and stews, yet it is delicate enough to include in savory loaves of bread.

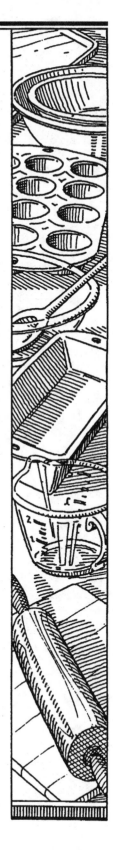

Black beans. Also called turtle beans, these shiny, kidney-shaped, black-skinned legumes are a staple in their native Cuba and in South and Central America. Today, black beans are also grown in the southern United States. They have a prominent flavor and a slightly mealy texture. Black beans are generally found in dried form. They can also be found canned in salt water. If using canned beans, be sure to first rinse them well.

Bouquet garni. This melange of dried herbs includes basil, oregano, thyme, marjoram, savory, rosemary, dill, tarragon, and sage. It can be used to season a wide variety of foods and breads.

Boursalt cheese. Imported from France, this *triple-crèmes* cheese has a delicate garlicky flavor and a rich, velvety consistency.

Boursin cheese. Boursin is perhaps the best known of the *triple-crèmes* cheeses. Imported from France, Boursin is a rich, soft, uncured cheese that has been infused with garlic; it has a delicate flavor and velvety consistency.

Bran. Bran is the coarse, dry outer layer of grains such as wheat, rye, and oats. Bran adds texture, fiber, and nutritional richness to breads and cereals. It also imparts a sweet, nutty flavor. For full nutritional value, be sure to buy unprocessed bran.

Bread flour. In contrast to pastry flour, which comes from soft wheat, bread flour comes from hard wheat and has a high protein and gluten content. Although it can be white or whole wheat, the bread flour called for in the recipes in this book is white bread flour because it is the most readily available. Supermarkets stock both varieties of white flour—pastry and bread—but their whole

wheat flour tends to have a low gluten content. Many natural foods stores stock both pastry and bread whole wheat flour. Although acceptable breads are made with other flours, the best breads are made with high-gluten bread flour. Gluten gives dough its elasticity and the strength it needs to expand and rise. It also makes bread crisp and chewy. Gluten can be added to any flour. (*See also* Gluten flour.)

Brie cheese. The best known of the cheeses imported from France, Brie is made from the whole milk of cows. It is the color of heavy cream and is encased in a reddish brown crust. With its superlative flavor and aggressive bouquet, a perfectly ripe Brie oozes slightly at room temperature.

Brown rice. Available in short-, medium-, and long-grain varieties, this tender and moist rice has a nutty flavor and texture. Because brown rice retains its bran coat and germ, it is slower to tenderize and takes longer to cook than do other rices. Brown rice is filled with protein, calcium, phosphorus, iron, vitamin E, and most of the B vitamins. When baking bread, the medium-grain variety is the best type to use.

Brown rice flour. This fine-textured flour is made from ground short- or medium-grain brown rice. It adds nutritional value to breads.

Buckwheat flour. While it has many of the characteristics of grains, buckwheat is actually a fruit with a high-quality protein balance, a rich concentration of iron, and a good supply of B vitamins and calcium. It is ideal for people who cannot tolerate wheat products. Buckwheat is ground into a finely milled flour. It can be found in

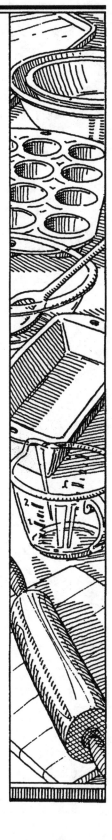

natural foods stores in light or dark varieties. Dark buckwheat flour is grayish with tiny black specks and contains about 17 percent of the hull. As buckwheat is not a grain, buckwheat flour does not contain gluten and must be used in conjunction with other flours in baking.

Bulghur. *See* Cracked wheat.

Buttermilk. Buttermilk, which was once a by-product of churned butter, is cultured from lowfat or nonfat milk. Although it does not have the thick consistency it once had, buttermilk retains its tangy tartness and adds a distinct flavor and light texture to breads.

Camembert cheese. Bearing the name of the village in Normandy where it is reputed to have first been made, Camembert is one of Europe's best-known French cheeses. Made from whole cow's milk, Camembert has a creamy yellow flesh that is encased in a speckled, floury, moldy-looking crust. A perfectly ripe Camembert is six weeks old and possesses a fruity, slightly tangy fragrance. It should be served at room temperature, when it is silky, spreadable, and aromatic.

Canola oil. A mild-flavored vegetable oil, canola is a good all-purpose oil. It is the lowest in polyunsaturated fat of any oil on the market. Following close behind in quality are safflower and sunflower oils. All three oils can be used interchangeably in the recipes in this book.

Caraway seeds. These seeds are a very popular European spice. They add flavor and crunch to many bread varieties. They are especially popular in rye breads.

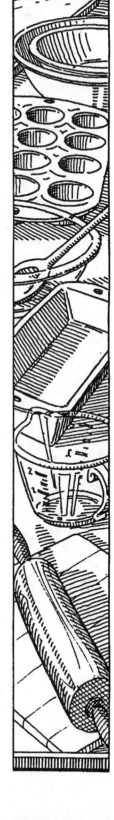

Cardamom. This member of the ginger family is native to India and is supplied encased in its pod. Remove the sweet, strong-flavored seeds from the pod and crush them before using them. Cardamom has a distinctive flavor but is commonly substituted for cinnamon. When buying whole cardamom, keep in mind that the palest pods contain the most flavorful seeds. Cardamom is also available ground, but ground cardamom loses its potency soon after the jar is opened.

Carob powder. This rich, sweet, dark brown powder comes from the dried pods of the honey locust tree. Because it contains less fat than chocolate and is not bitter (thus requiring less sweetener than chocolate does), it is often used as a healthful alternative. It can be substituted in equal amounts for cocoa powder in any recipe.

Celery seeds. These tiny, olive-brown seeds are obtained from wild celery plants. Their flavor is almost identical to, though more intense than, that of celery.

Cheddar cheese. Wisconsin, New York, and Vermont produce the best American Cheddars, which range from very mild to very sharp. New York, once the primary Cheddar producer, prides itself on a dry, crumbly Cheddar with a sharp, full flavor that is substantial enough to be noticed when baked in breads. A sharp Cheddar is recommended in whole-grain baked goods, so that the flavor is not overpowered.

Cheshire cheese. Probably the oldest cheese made in Britain, blue-veined Cheshire ranges in color from pale yellow to warm apricot. It has a rich, mellow flavor and a moist, crumbly texture. A sharp Cheddar can be substituted for Cheshire in any recipe.

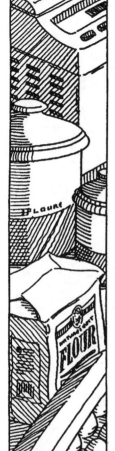

Chèvre cheese. Also referred to simply as goat cheese, chèvre has a buttery consistency and a unique bouquet. When young, the cheese is soft and has a gentle aroma. With age, the texture becomes drier and the flavor more dominant.

Chick peas. These round, tan-colored beans come from the Mediterranean region and the Middle East. They are called chick peas because each bean has a small peak that resembles a chicken's beak. They are also known as garbanzo beans or ceci beans. Chick peas possess a nutty, earthy flavor and are very versatile. Not available fresh, they are found dry or, more commonly, canned in salt water. Be sure to rinse the canned beans well before using them.

Chilies. The little peppers called chilies come in many varieties, but all contribute color, flavor, piquancy, and a degree of heat to food. They can range from mild to very hot, from sweet to quite acidic, and from fresh to dried. While there are over a hundred varieties of chilies, only a few are readily available in supermarkets. The fresh green or red chilies have a crisp, grassy taste, while the dried ones are musky and a bit fruity. Jalapeño chilies are found fresh, canned, or jarred. Fresh, these chilies should be firm and unblemished with unbroken skin. If using canned chilies, transfer any unused peppers to a jar with an airtight cover and store in the refrigerator; they will keep for several months. Small, narrow, hot dried red chilies called *pepperoncini rossi* are available whole or crumbled and packed in jars. For maximum potency, these chilies should be used within three months of opening the jar.

Chili powder is a blend of ground chili peppers, cumin, oregano, garlic, and salt. Depending on whether it is mild or hot, it will add

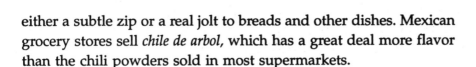

either a subtle zip or a real jolt to breads and other dishes. Mexican grocery stores sell *chile de arbol,* which has a great deal more flavor than the chili powders sold in most supermarkets.

Chocolate. Chocolate is made from the beans of the cacao tree, an evergreen tree of the cola family. This tree is native to the tropical Amazon forests. Chocolate is a mixture of roasted cocoa, cocoa butter, and very fine sugar. Unsweetened (or bitter) chocolate is available in squares and is the natural rich chocolate ground from the cocoa beans. It has a full-bodied flavor and is ideal for baking and cooking. Semisweet chocolate, available in bits and morsels, is chocolate that has been processed with sugar and viscose to make it syrupy when melted. Cocoa comes in powdered form and is made from roasted cocoa beans. It is unsweetened, and its flavor is bitter.

Cinnamon. Cinnamon is native to the East Indies and southeast Asia. This sweet aromatic spice is made from the dried inner bark of certain trees (*Cinnamomum zeylanicum* and *C. cassia*). Cinnamon comes in many forms, from powder to chips to rolled sticks. As cinnamon loses its aromatic intensity after about three months, it should be purchased in small amounts. Ground cinnamon must be used with caution when making breads, as it tends to counter the rising ability of yeast.

Cocoa. *See* Chocolate.

Coriander. Also called cilantro or Chinese parsley, coriander is a pink-flowered native of southern Europe. In its fresh form, it resembles flat-leaf (Italian) parsley. Minty-fresh, aromatic, and utterly captivating, this strong herb lends a noticeable flavor to

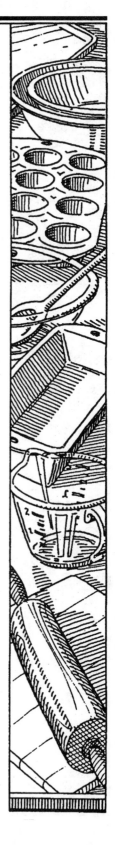

breads. Coriander seeds are dried and ground; they are used in Middle Eastern–style dishes.

Cornmeal. Cornmeal comes in three colors: yellow, white, and blue. Look for stone-ground meals, which contain the flavorful germ, lost in many of the supermarket varieties. Yellow cornmeal retains more carotene than the white and is generally more flavorful, but for the most part, the two are interchangeable.

Cottage cheese. Made from skim milk, with cream possibly added, cottage cheese's most noticeable characteristic is its texture. Its tender curds create a soft, slightly lumpy consistency, yet it is firm enough to hold its shape. Creamy white with a pleasant, slightly tangy flavor, cottage cheese has a delicate aroma.

Cracked wheat. Consisting of whole wheat kernels that have been cracked or cut into pieces, this coarse grain adds fiber and substance to breads, cereals, and casseroles. Cracked wheat is raw and needs at least 15 minutes of cooking before it can be used. Bulghur, which is cracked wheat that has been steamed, needs just a soaking before it is used.

Cream cheese. Generally found in rectangular white blocks, cream cheese is made from a mixture of cream and milk. Today, most have a minimum fat content of 33 percent. This silky, smooth cheese with its refined, slightly acidic flavor is often infused with gum arabic, a stabilizer. Search out the brands without this additive. They have a lighter, more natural texture, although their storage life is somewhat shorter.

Cumin. A member of the parsley family, cumin hails from Egypt, where it grows as a small plant bearing umbels of small rose or white flowers and produces fruit and cumin seeds. Most often used in its ground form, cumin's sharp, strong, and earthy taste is used to add range and depth to many Middle Eastern–style dishes. Cumin is often paired with coriander to produce breads with decidedly Middle Eastern undertones. Cumin seeds look very much like caraway seeds but have a flavor of their own. Cumin adds a prominent chili flavor to breads, but because of its strong nature, it must be used with caution.

Currants. Currants are the small dried berries of a spineless shrub that is native to the Mediterranean region. While fresh currants are available in July, dried ones are preferred for bread baking.

Curry. A mixture of many spices, including turmeric, ground cumin, and cardamom, curry adds a sweet, distinctive flavor and yellow color to the breads and dishes in which it is used.

Dates. Dates come packaged in a number of different forms. Pitted and unpitted dates from the Middle East and California are sold in plastic containers and are unsweetened. Chopped dates that have been rolled in powdered sugar are much sweeter. For the recipes in this book, I suggest using the unsweetened variety.

Date sugar is ground from dehydrated dates and is not actually a sugar. It is high in fiber and rich in vitamins, minerals, and iron. Date sugar can be used in baking when a textured sweetener is required.

Dill. Originally discovered in southern Europe, dill has since been transplanted to more northern climates. Another member of the

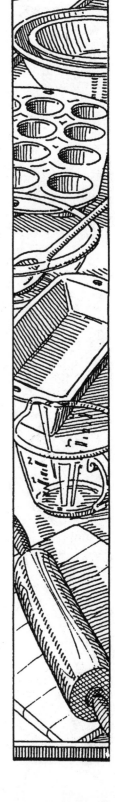

very large parsley clan, the dill plant has bitter seeds and skinny, aromatic leaves. This licorice-tasting herb can often be found in the supermarket, especially during the summer months. Its leaves and seeds are also available dried and should be stored in jars. The dried leaves are an especially nice addition to delicate breads, while the seeds can be crushed and added to hearty whole-grain breads.

Emmenthaler. This is one of Switzerland's two great cheeses for melting (Gruyère is the other). Emmenthaler is a true Swiss cheese, with a characteristically full, nutty flavor and a delicate goldenrod color. Riddled with holes (or eyes), this cheese grates well and melts into characteristic long strings. When buying this exceptional cheese, be sure the rind is stamped in red with the word "Switzerland" to prove its authenticity.

Farmer cheese. Once sold only in bulk, this part-skim cow's milk cheese now can be found packaged in smaller quantities. Its flavor is milky clean, full, and slightly sour; its texture is similar to lightly crumbled cream cheese. Avoid farmer cheese that has a firm slicing texture.

Fennel seeds. With a bright, pungent flavor that hints of licorice, fennel seeds add crunch and character to whole-grain breads.

Feta cheese. Originally made by shepherds, this sheep's milk cheese is soft, salty, and strong flavored. It is white and crumbly yet firm enough to hold its shape when cooked. Essential in the cuisines of Greece and the Balkans, feta comes packed in brine. To retard the aging process, the brine should be replaced with a mixture of equal parts water and milk that has been boiled and then cooled.

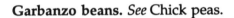

Garbanzo beans. *See* Chick peas.

Garlic. This fragrant bulb, available in many forms, adds a gentle aroma and pronounced taste to breads. Fresh garlic should be plump and firm with the papery skin firmly attached. It should not be refrigerated but rather stored in a cool, dry place with good ventilation. Chopped or minced fresh garlic that has been preserved in oil and sealed in jars is also available; this garlic has a clean, crisp taste and is convenient to use. The least desirable form of garlic is the powdered type.

Ginger. Stored in glass jars, the powdered form of ginger root is readily available in supermarkets. Ginger adds a pleasant aroma and faint, spicy taste to breads when combined with other spices.

Gluten flour. As the gluten content of many whole-grain flours is low, it is often necessary to supplement the flour by adding wheat gluten to the dough. Gluten is available in natural foods stores and can add height, lightness, and a small amount of protein to your breads.

Graham flour. This whole wheat flour has had the inner portion of its kernels finely ground. The bran layers are then returned to the flour, giving it a coarse, flaky texture. When purchasing graham flour, be sure it still contains the germ. It is excellent for rolls and breads.

Gruyère cheese. Gruyère is one of Switzerland's great cheeses for melting. This cow's milk cheese has brown, wrinkled skin covering deep ivory-colored flesh. Gruyère is a deep, nutty, and full-flavored cheese with a hint of sweetness.

Havarti cheese. Made from cow's milk, this exciting, creamy cheese has small irregular holes dotting its landscape. Mild yet tangy, rindless Havarti comes either plain or flavored with dill, chives, caraway, or other herbs or spices.

Honey. Cooking with honey has become so commonplace that the many colors and flavors of this sweetener are often overlooked. Honey ranges in color from ash white to dark amber, with flavors from mild to quite pronounced. When sugar is used in a bread, it can be identified only by its sweetness. Honey on the other hand adds flavor as well as subtle color. Honey, molasses, and maple syrup are the preferred sweeteners in whole-grain baking.

Jarlsberg cheese. A hard-pressed cow's milk cheese from Norway, Jarlsberg has many of the characteristics of Gruyère and Emmenthaler. It has a straw-colored interior that is dotted with large holes, and it has a firm, smooth, and elastic texture.

Lemon zest. *See* Zest.

Mace. This spice is made from the dried, waxy covering that partly encloses the kernel of the nutmeg. Mace's flavor is similar to nutmeg and is used in whole or ground form.

Maple syrup. A simple carbohydrate, maple syrup is the boiled-down sap of the sugar maple tree. Not quite as sweet as honey, maple syrup has a more distinctive flavor and about 15 percent less calories.

Milk (dry). Instant nonfat dry milk is skim milk in a granular form. It is a top-quality milk with only the fat and water removed. Used

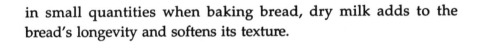

in small quantities when baking bread, dry milk adds to the bread's longevity and softens its texture.

Milk (liquid). Skim, lowfat, or whole milk can be used interchangeably in the recipes in this book. Milk adds a significant amount of protein and minerals to breads; it also creates a subtle difference in texture. Be sure to scald your milk before using it, so that the milk does not deactivate the yeast's gluten properties. To scald milk, simply heat it just to the boiling point (a skin will form).

Molasses. The cooked liquid that remains after the crystallization of granulated sugar is called molasses, and it is a common ingredient in baked products. Molasses lends a noticeable flavor and color to baked goods, the intensity of which depend on the type of molasses used. Blackstrap molasses is the strongest in taste and has the most intense color. It also contains the most iron, calcium, potassium, and B vitamins. Because of its very noticeable color, however, blackstrap molasses should be used only in very dark breads. The light-colored molasses varieties are better suited for most breads.

Mint. This almost indestructible plant has the ability to grow under deplorable conditions. Since it is so easily grown, there is little excuse for using dried mint, which has a decidedly bitter taste. Fresh mint's subtle flavor has a Mediterranean flair.

Mozzarella cheese. At one time, mozzarella was made solely from buffalo's milk, and in some parts of southern Italy it still is. Today, the majority of mozzarella, whether fresh or prepackaged, is made from cow's milk. Served as a table cheese or in salads, versatile mozzarella is often used as a topping on pizza and breads.

Muenster cheese. A rich, smooth cheese with a creamy white interior and orange rind, Muenster is fairly mild in flavor and aroma when young. With age, this cheese turns a buttercup yellow and takes on a more distinctive air.

Oat-blend flour. A blend of wheat and oat flours, this flour retains most of the nutrients present in whole oats, as the bran and germ have not been removed. Oat-blend flour adds significant amounts of iron, calcium, and phosphorus to breads.

Oat bran. Finely ground from whole oat groats, oat bran is used as a nutty, flavorful cereal. Included in baked products, it adds fiber.

Oats. Oats come in many varieties—instant, quick-cooking, and rolled (the long-cooking variety). Rolled oats, which are whole oats with the husks removed, are the type most commonly used in baking. First steamed and then flattened between rollers, rolled oats are used in cereals, cakes, cookies, and breads. Toasting the flakes enhances their flavor. Rolled oats can also be placed in a blender or food processor and ground to a finer consistency before being incorporated in a recipe.

Orange zest. *See* Zest.

Oregano. The Mediterranean influence comes through loud and clear in the lusty, potent impact of this popular herb. Oregano adds a very noticeable Italian flavor to all types of breads.

Peanut butter. Ground from whole peanuts, this familiar spread is high in protein. Unfortunately, it is also high in fat. I suggest using natural peanut butter, without added sugar, oil, or salt.

Pont L'Eveque cheese. This cheese comes in small plump squares, each with a scented, cross-hatched surface. Inside, this exceptional cheese is a pale creamy yellow and laced with tiny holes. A soft, melting texture and an amazingly deep, vibrant flavor make this one of France's finest cheeses.

Popcorn flour. A powder-soft flour ground from popped kernels of corn, popcorn flour is something you must make yourself. Pop unflavored, unsalted popcorn, then grind the cooled popped kernels in a blender or food processor until fine. This flour can be stored the same way you store all your flours. Approximately $3^{1}/_{2}$ ounces of unpopped corn yield 4 cups of unpacked flour.

Poppy seeds. Originally from Holland, these tiny, dark seeds of the poppy flower are quite fragrant. Poppy seeds are used more for their crunch than their flavor and are found in and on top of many breads and rolls.

Port du Salut cheese. Also called Port Salut, this cheese is mild flavored and has a creamy texture. Its flavor, however smooth, is robust, which sets it apart from other bland cheeses. Its mellowness blends well with sweets, fruits, and hearty dark breads.

Pumpernickel flour. *See* Rye meal.

Raisins. In the United States, California produces the finest raisins, in gold and black varieties. Raisins add a delicious dimension to breads and rolls.

Ricotta cheese. This whey cheese comes fresh in wet white curds that are similar to, though somewhat finer than, those of cottage cheese. Ricotta has a mild, slightly sweet flavor and no aroma.

Roquefort cheese. This internationally famous French blue cheese is made from the milk of sheep. It has a firm yet slightly crumbly texture and a powdery white flesh that is laced with characteristic green-blue veins. It is difficult to describe the incredible flavor of a true Roquefort. Even though it is crumbly, the cheese is even and smooth, and its taste is mellow with a sophisticated piquancy.

Rosemary. Rosemary plants grow wild in the Mediterranean and produce clusters of small, light blue flowers and leaves that are used in many dishes. This extremely pungent herb is most often found dried in its whole or crumbled leaf form. When rosemary is in prime condition, it imparts a fresh, woodsy flavor and odor. It is perfect in Italian flat breads.

Rye flour. Ground from whole rye berries, rye flour is sold in white-, medium-, and dark-colored varieties. The medium-colored flour is the one most commonly used to make delicious breads, rolls, and crackers. However, because of rye flour's low gluten content, it must be combined with other flours in order for the bread to rise properly.

Rye meal. Often called pumpernickel flour, rye meal is actually coarsely ground whole rye flour. This "flour" has the consistency of cornmeal and is usually combined with rye flour and whole wheat flour to make pumpernickel and other dark breads.

Safflower oil. *See* Canola oil.

Saffron. Orange-colored saffron threads are the dried stigmas from a plant of the iris family. Although saffron is quite expensive, a little bit goes a long way in flavoring rice dishes, sauces, soups, and

breads. Saffron adds a deep yellow color to any dish, as well as to fingers and wooden spoons, so be careful.

Sage. Long known as a medicinal herb, sage is also used to flavor soups, cheeses, and baked goods. Sage has an interesting, woodsy flavor and aroma. It is often used in combination with other herbs and spices.

Semolina. Semolina is a refined durum wheat flour. Because the bran and germ have been sifted out, semolina is very light in color and texture, resulting in airy breads and pastas.

Sesame seeds. The flat, oval seeds of an East Indian plant, sesame seeds add flavor and crunch to baked products. They have a rich, warm flavor, which can be enhanced by toasting.

Soy flakes. These large flakes are made from whole soybeans that are toasted for about 30 seconds, then flaked in a roller mill. Soy flakes have all the qualities of whole soybeans, with the advantage of being easier and faster to cook. They add nutrition and texture to baked products.

Soy flour. This high-protein flour is made from raw soybeans that have been hulled, cracked, and finely ground. As soy flour has a distinctive flavor, it usually makes up less than 25 percent of the total flour content in a bread recipe. Soy flour adds valuable vitamins, calcium, and iron to breads.

Soy margarine. Pure soy margarine contains soybean oil, soybeans, salt, vegetable lecithin, and water. It can be used interchangeably with canola, safflower, and sunflower oil.

Swiss cheese. The universal success of Switzerland's Emmenthaler has inspired virtually every country that makes cheese to create its own domestic variety. Many types are uninspiring and not worth mentioning. Others, such as the Swiss cheese that is produced in Wisconsin, are worthy of consideration. The major problem with most Swiss cheeses is a lack of sufficient aging. A good Swiss should be white or a slightly glossy cream color. It should have a mild, nutty sweet taste and should be riddled with shiny holes. If not purchasing Emmenthaler, take care to select a Swiss that has been aged at least 60 days. (*See also* Emmenthaler; Gruyère cheese; Jarlsberg cheese.)

Sun-dried tomatoes. Adding a unique quality to many Italian-style breads and pasta dishes, sun-dried tomatoes are experiencing a well-deserved popularity. Their unusual, intense flavor is far removed from that of a fresh tomato. The best sun-dried tomatoes, which are packed in olive oil, come from Italy. Since domestic farmers are beginning to produce them, dry sun-dried tomatoes can be found in the produce section of many supermarkets.

To reconstitute dry sun-dried tomatoes, simply place them in a pan with water to cover. Bring the water to a boil, then reduce the heat and simmer the tomatoes until they are soft (about 30 minutes). Allow to cool, then transfer the tomatoes along with the cooking water to a clean airtight jar. Add 2 tablespoons of olive oil for every 3 ounces of dried tomatoes. Cover tightly and place in the refrigerator, where they will keep for up to 6 months.

Sunflower oil. *See* Canola oil.

Taco seasoning. A combination of herbs and spices including oregano and chili powder, this spicy seasoning is available in individual packages and adds a Mexican flavor to breads.

Tahini. Made from hulled sesame seeds, this paste has a consistency thinner than that of peanut butter. It can be found in natural foods stores and in the international-foods section of most supermarkets. Once you open a can or jar of tahini, keep it refrigerated.

Thyme. During the summer months in France, hillsides are fragrant with an abundance of thyme. An essential ingredient in French cuisine, thyme has crossed the ocean to add a sharp, warm, and pungent touch to American dishes as well. A pinch of thyme, particularly when paired with other herbs, makes a flavorful addition to a loaf of bread.

VegeBase. This organic vegetable blend is made of soybeans, carrots, peas, onion, spinach, celery, parsnips, kale, parsley, vegetable oil, vegetable proteins, and herbal seasonings. It comes in powdered form and, when mixed with boiling water, makes a wonderful broth. It is available in natural foods stores.

Walnuts. A delicious crunchy addition to many baked goods, the walnut's pleasant bitterness benefits from toasting before the nut is added to bread dough.

Wheat germ. The most nutritious part of the wheat berry, wheat germ can be eaten raw or toasted. It is often added to baked goods to provide fiber and a crunchy texture. Be sure to refrigerate an opened jar of wheat germ, as the germ contains oils that quickly turn rancid at room temperature.

Whole wheat flour. Unlike white flour, which is made from only the starchy endosperm portion of the wheat kernel, whole wheat flour is made from the whole kernel, including the germ and bran.

Whole wheat flour therefore has more nutrients, more fiber, and a more complex flavor than white flour. There are two types of whole wheat flour: pastry flour, which comes from low-gluten soft wheat, and bread flour, which comes from hard wheat and has the strength and elasticity that benefit bread. The whole wheat flour commonly available in supermarkets is pastry flour, which has a low gluten content. When I make bread, I use whole wheat bread flour, and that is what is meant when a recipe in this book calls for whole wheat flour. You can substitute whole wheat pastry flour, but the resulting bread will be heavier and denser.

Yeast. Yeast is a simple one-celled plant that is the leavening agent for cakes and breads. When added to certain ingredients under proper conditions, yeast grows rapidly, forming the gas that makes breads and cakes light and airy. For more information on yeast, see pages 8–9.

Yogurt. This nutritious food is made by introducing a harmless bacteria into milk and allowing it to feed on the milk sugars. This creates a slight acidity that makes yogurt a thick and tangy food, high in nutritional value. It adds a light, airy texture to breads.

Zest. The zest from oranges and lemons is actually the coarse outer rind of the fruit. (Only the colored part of the rind, not the bitter inner white portion, contains the flavor.) Zest should be grated and used whenever the distinct flavor of lemon or orange is desired. Dried zest, which is found in the spice section of most supermarkets, should be kept on hand for emergencies. Freshly grated zest has no equal. When lemons and oranges are in season, buy a large quantity and make your own zest. Cut the fruits in half and squeeze out the fresh juice, reserving it for another use. With a

sharp knife or potato peeler, remove the outer rind from the fruit and coarsely grind it in a blender or food processor. Place the ground zest in a heavy-duty plastic bag and keep it in the freezer, where it will stay fresh for up to a year.

CHAPTER 2

Whole Wheat
& Gluten Breads

hole-grain baking can be as varied and diverse as your imagination, but this type of baking almost always begins with the same basic ingredient: whole wheat. Just as breadmaking began with wheat many centuries ago, so does today's automatic breadmaking. Whole wheat flour provides the basis for most of the recipes in this book, although it is often combined with other flours for added nutritional value, texture, and taste. This chapter offers recipes for light, moist, and savory breads that showcase wheat's distinctive flavor and aroma. Also included are a few recipes that utilize bread flour with its high gluten content. Instructions for making pizza dough and dough for soft-baked pretzels are also presented.

This chapter is the perfect place to begin your adventure into the world of breadmaking. It offers many simple basic bread recipes that are designed to help you become familiar with your bread machine. A handful of more complicated recipes is also included for those times when you feel up for a challenge. No matter which recipe you choose, you will delight in the fabulous tastes and aromas that only freshly baked bread can bring.

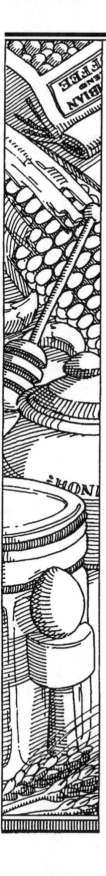

$\mathcal{S}$imple Whole Wheat Bread

INGREDIENT	1-POUND LOAF	1^1/$_2$-POUND LOAF
Whole wheat flour	2^1/$_4$ cups	2^2/$_3$ cups
Gluten flour	^{1}/$_4$ cup	^{1}/$_3$ cup
Dry milk	1 tablespoon	1^1/$_2$ tablespoons
Sea salt	1 teaspoon	1^1/$_2$ teaspoons
Water	1 cup	1^1/$_4$ cups
Honey	2 tablespoons	3 tablespoons
Canola, safflower, or sunflower oil	1 tablespoon	1^1/$_2$ tablespoons
Active dry yeast	1 package	4 teaspoons

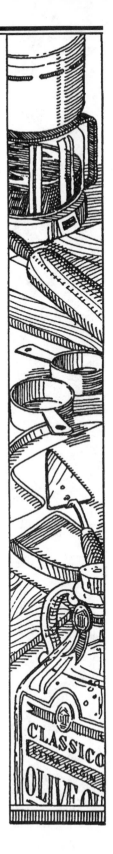

*An uncomplicated bread that highlights
wheat's unique flavor.*

1. Fit the kneading blade firmly
on the shaft in the bread pan. Carefully measure the dry
ingredients and transfer to the pan. Add the liquid ingredients
and the yeast. Place the bread pan inside the machine and close
the lid.

2. Program the breadmaker for
the whole wheat mode. The unit will begin its operation.

3. At the end of the baking cycle,
remove the bread promptly from the machine, taking care, as the
oven surfaces will be very hot. Invert the bread pan onto a wire
rack and shake several times to dislodge the bread. Allow to cool
completely on the rack before slicing or wrapping for storage.

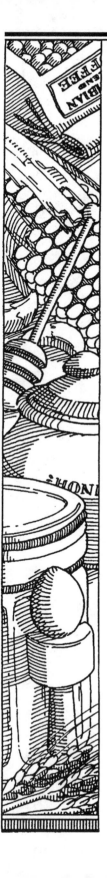

Whole Wheat and Popcorn Bread

INGREDIENT	1-POUND LOAF	1^1/2-POUND LOAF
Whole wheat flour	2^1/4 cups	2^2/3 cups
Popcorn flour	^{1}/2 cup	^{1}/2 cup
Gluten flour	1^1/2 tablespoons	^{1}/4 cup
Dry milk	1 tablespoon	1^1/2 tablespoons
Sea salt	1 teaspoon	1^1/2 teaspoons
Water	1 cup	1^1/4 cups
Soy margarine	2 tablespoons	3 tablespoons
Molasses	1 tablespoon	1^1/2 tablespoons
Honey	1 tablespoon	1 tablespoon
Active dry yeast	1 package	4 teaspoons

Popcorn flour lightens this loaf and provides added nutrients, while the honey and molasses give the bread an interesting hint of sweetness.

1. Fit the kneading blade firmly on the shaft in the bread pan. Carefully measure the dry ingredients and transfer to the pan. Add the liquid ingredients and the yeast. Place the bread pan inside the machine and close the lid.

2. Program the breadmaker for the whole wheat mode. The unit will begin its operation.

3. At the end of the baking cycle, remove the bread promptly from the machine, taking care, as the oven surfaces will be very hot. Invert the bread pan onto a wire rack and shake several times to dislodge the bread. Allow to cool completely on the rack before slicing or wrapping for storage.

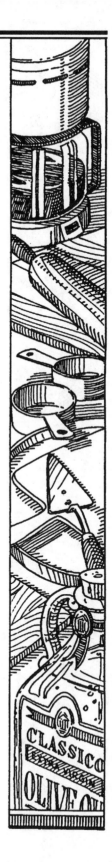

*B*lackstrap Bread

INGREDIENT	1-POUND LOAF	1½-POUND LOAF
Whole wheat flour	2¼ cups	2⅔ cups
Whole rye flour	¼ cup	⅓ cup
Soy flakes	2 tablespoons	3 tablespoons
Gluten flour	2 tablespoons	3 tablespoons
Ground caraway seeds	1 tablespoon	1½ tablespoons
Sea salt	1 teaspoon	1½ teaspoons
Grated lemon zest	½ teaspoon	¾ teaspoon
Cold coffee	1 cup plus 2 tablespoons	1¼ cups plus 3 tablespoons
Canola, safflower, or sunflower oil	1 tablespoon	1½ tablespoons
Blackstrap molasses	2 teaspoons	1 tablespoon
Active dry yeast	1 package	4 teaspoons

Top: **Sun-Dried Tomato and Rosemary Bread (page 66)**
Bottom: **Focaccia (page 52)**

Top: Sun-Dried Tomato and Rosemary Bread (page 66)
Top: Rosemary Pita Pockets (page 60)
   With Cucumber and Yogurt Dip (page 286)
Bottom: Pita Pockets (page 58) Stuffed With Garden Vegetables

*A hearty loaf with a pronounced flavor, this interesting
bread blends wheat and rye flours, strong coffee,
blackstrap molasses, and a hint of spices.*

1. Fit the kneading blade firmly on the shaft in the bread pan. Carefully measure the dry ingredients and transfer to the pan. Add the liquid ingredients and the yeast. Place the bread pan inside the machine and close the lid.

2. Program the breadmaker for the whole wheat mode. The unit will begin its operation.

3. At the end of the baking cycle, remove the bread promptly from the machine, taking care, as the oven surfaces will be very hot. Invert the bread pan onto a wire rack and shake several times to dislodge the bread. Allow to cool completely on the rack before slicing or wrapping for storage.

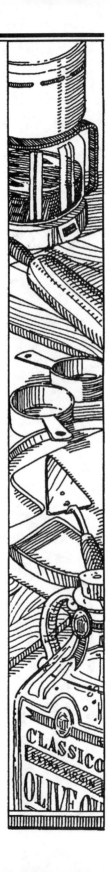

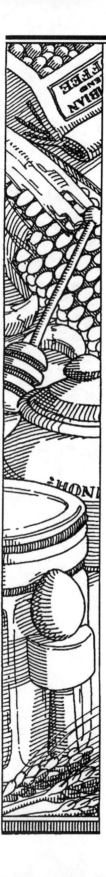

Brown Rice Bread

INGREDIENT	1-POUND LOAF	1^1/$_2$-POUND LOAF
Whole wheat flour	2 cups	2^1/$_3$ cups
Brown rice flour	^{1}/$_4$ cup	^{1}/$_3$ cup
Gluten flour	^{1}/$_4$ cup	^{1}/$_3$ cup
Dry milk	1 tablespoon	1^1/$_2$ tablespoons
Water	1 cup	1^1/$_4$ cups
Honey	2 tablespoons	2^1/$_2$ tablespoons
Canola, safflower, or sunflower oil	1 tablespoon	1^1/$_2$ tablespoons
Active dry yeast	1 package	4 teaspoons

*Wheat and brown rice flour and the nutty chewiness
of cooked brown rice give this fragrant bread a wallop
of nutrition in every slice.*

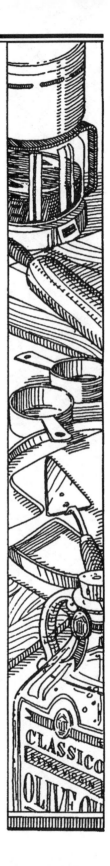

1. Fit the kneading blade firmly
on the shaft in the bread pan. Carefully measure the dry
ingredients and transfer to the pan. Add the liquid ingredients
and yeast. Place the bread pan inside the machine and close the
lid.

2. Program the breadmaker for
the whole wheat mode. The unit will begin its operation.

3. At the end of the baking cycle,
remove the bread promptly from the machine, taking care, as the
oven surfaces will be very hot. Invert the bread pan onto a wire
rack and shake several times to dislodge the bread. Allow to cool
completely on the rack before slicing or wrapping for storage.

Corn Wheat Bread

INGREDIENT	1-POUND LOAF	1^1/$_2$-POUND LOAF
Whole wheat flour	2 cups	2^1/$_3$ cups
Yellow cornmeal	^{1}/$_4$ cup	^{1}/$_3$ cup
Whole rye flour	2 tablespoons	3 tablespoons
Gluten flour	2 tablespoons	3 tablespoons
Date sugar	1 tablespoon	1^1/$_2$ tablespoons
Minced fresh rosemary, or dried rosemary	1 tablespoon 1 teaspoon	1^1/$_2$ tablespoons 1^1/$_2$ teaspoons
Dry milk	1 tablespoon	1 tablespoon
Sea salt	1 teaspoon	1^1/$_2$ teaspoons
Water	^{7}/$_8$ cup	1^1/$_4$ cups
Plain nonfat yogurt	2 tablespoons	3 tablespoons
Canola, safflower, or sunflower oil	1 tablespoon	1 tablespoon
Active dry yeast	1 package	4 teaspoons

This bread has a slightly grainy texture from the addition of cornmeal and a very savory aroma from the rosemary.

1. Fit the kneading blade firmly on the shaft in the bread pan. Carefully measure the dry ingredients and transfer to the pan. Add the liquid ingredients and the yeast. Place the bread pan inside the machine and close the lid.

2. Program the breadmaker for the whole wheat mode. The unit will begin its operation.

3. At the end of the baking cycle, remove the bread promptly from the machine, taking care, as the oven surfaces will be very hot. Invert the bread pan onto a wire rack and shake several times to dislodge the bread. Allow to cool completely on the rack before slicing or wrapping for storage.

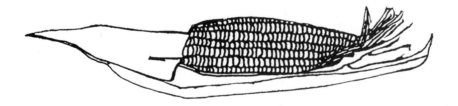

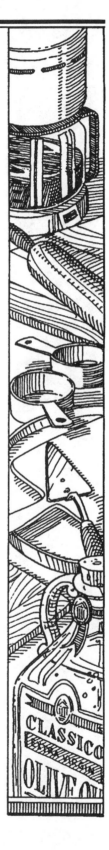

 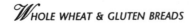

Cuban Bread

INGREDIENT	1-POUND LOAF	1¹/₂-POUND LOAF
Potato, peeled and quartered	1 medium	1 medium
Water	1¹/₂ cups	1¹/₂ cups
Whole wheat flour	1¹/₄ cups	1¹/₂ cups
Bread flour	1¹/₄ cups	1¹/₂ cups
Sea salt	1 teaspoon	1¹/₂ teaspoons
Date sugar	1 teaspoon	1¹/₂ teaspoons
Canola, safflower, or sunflower oil	1 tablespoon	2 tablespoons
Active dry yeast	1 package	4 teaspoons
Yellow cornmeal	1 tablespoon	1¹/₂ tablespoons

What makes this simple bread different is the way it is baked. Brushing the bread with cold water while it is baking in the oven makes the loaf crisp. The bread is marvelous served hot, straight from the oven.

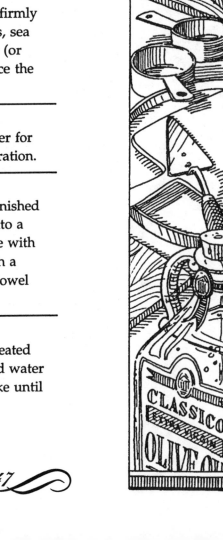

1. In a small pot, combine the potato quarters and the water, and bring to a boil. Reduce the heat and simmer until the potato quarters are tender, about 10 minutes. Remove the potato quarters and either discard or save for another use. Set the liquid aside to cool.

2. Fit the kneading blade firmly on the shaft in the bread pan. Carefully measure the flours, sea salt, and sugar, and transfer to the pan. Add the oil, 1 cup (or 1^1/4 cups) of the reserved potato water, and the yeast. Place the bread pan inside the machine and close the lid.

3. Program the breadmaker for the whole wheat dough mode. The unit will begin its operation.

4. When the dough has finished rising, turn it out onto a lightly floured surface. Form it into a long loaf. Lightly coat a baking sheet with oil and sprinkle with the cornmeal. Place the loaf in the center of the sheet. With a sharp knife, slash the top in 6 places. Cover with a clean towel and let rise for 20 minutes.

5. Bake the loaf in a preheated 400°F oven for 10 minutes. Lightly brush the top with cold water and bake 10 minutes more. Brush the bread again and bake until golden, about 15 minutes more. Serve hot.

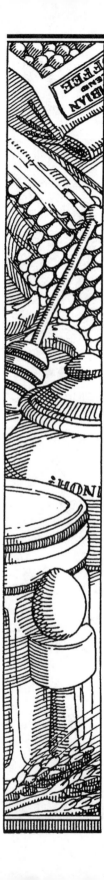

English Toasted Bread

INGREDIENT	1-POUND LOAF	1¹/₂-POUND LOAF
Warm water	$^5/_8$ cup	$^7/_8$ cup
Baking soda	$^1/_2$ teaspoon	$^3/_4$ teaspoon
Bread flour	$2^1/_4$ cups	3 cups
Dry milk	2 tablespoons	3 tablespoons
Sea salt	1 teaspoon	$1^1/_2$ teaspoons
Sourdough Starter (see page 78)	$^1/_2$ cup	$^3/_4$ cup
Canola, safflower, or sunflower oil	1 tablespoon	$1^1/_2$ tablespoons
Honey	1 teaspoon	2 teaspoons
Active dry yeast	2 teaspoons	1 package

Perfect for slathering with homemade jam, this sourdough bread has much of the texture of an English muffin.

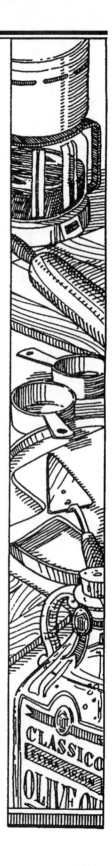

1. In a small cup, combine the warm water and baking soda, and set aside for 5 minutes.

2. Fit the kneading blade firmly on the shaft in the bread pan. Carefully measure the flour, dry milk, and salt, and transfer to the pan. Add the Sourdough Starter, water–baking soda mixture, oil, honey, and yeast. Place the bread pan inside the machine and close the lid.

3. Program the breadmaker for the whole wheat mode. The unit will begin its operation.

4. At the end of the baking cycle, remove the bread promptly from the machine, taking care, as the oven surfaces will be very hot. Invert the bread pan onto a wire rack and shake several times to dislodge the bread. Allow to cool completely on the rack before slicing or wrapping for storage.

Fiesta Bread

INGREDIENT	1-POUND LOAF	1^1/$_2$-POUND LOAF
Whole wheat flour	1^1/$_2$ cups	1^3/$_4$ cups
Bread flour	1 cup	1^1/$_4$ cups
Taco seasoning	3^1/$_2$ tablespoons	5 tablespoons
Dry milk	1 tablespoon	1^1/$_2$ tablespoons
Sea salt	^{1}/$_2$ teaspoon	1 teaspoon
Water	1 cup	1^1/$_4$ cups
Olive oil	1 tablespoon	2 tablespoons
Honey	1 tablespoon	1 tablespoon
Active dry yeast	1 package	4 teaspoons

A perfect bread to accompany Mexican-inspired dishes, this rosy loaf gets its flavor and color from the taco seasoning.

1. Fit the kneading blade firmly on the shaft in the bread pan. Carefully measure the dry ingredients and transfer to the pan. Add the liquid ingredients and the yeast. Place the bread pan inside the machine and close the lid.

2. Program the breadmaker for the whole wheat mode. The unit will begin its operation.

3. At the end of the baking cycle, remove the bread promptly from the machine, taking care, as the oven surfaces will be very hot. Invert the bread pan onto a wire rack and shake several times to dislodge the bread. Allow to cool completely on the rack before slicing or wrapping for storage.

Focaccia

INGREDIENT	1-POUND LOAF	$1^{1}/2$-POUND LOAF
Garlic	3 cloves	4 cloves
Whole wheat flour	$1^{3}/4$ cups	2 cups
Bread flour	$^{3}/4$ cup	1 cup
Dry milk	1 tablespoon	$1^{1}/2$ tablespoons
Sea salt	1 teaspoon	$1^{1}/2$ teaspoons
Water	1 cup	$1^{1}/4$ cups
Olive oil	$^{1}/4$ cup	$^{1}/4$ cup plus 2 tablespoons
Honey	1 teaspoon	$1^{1}/2$ teaspoons
Active dry yeast	1 package	4 teaspoons
Minced fresh basil, or dried basil	1 tablespoon 1 teaspoon	2 tablespoons 2 teaspoons
Minced fresh rosemary, or dried rosemary	1 teaspoon $^{1}/2$ teaspoon	2 teaspoons 1 teaspoon

The Italians make a wonderful flat bread that can be easily started in your bread machine. Its flavors are enhanced not only by the garlic in the dough itself but by being brushed with garlic, oil, and herbs before baking.

1. Fit the kneading blade firmly on the shaft in the bread pan. Crush one of the garlic cloves and place it in the pan along with the flours, milk, salt, water, 1 tablespoon (or 2 tablespoons) of the olive oil, honey, and yeast. Place the bread pan inside the machine and close the lid.

2. Program the breadmaker for the whole wheat dough mode. The unit will begin its operation.

3. At the end of the rising cycle, turn the dough out onto a lightly floured surface. Divide the dough into 2 pieces, cover, and let rest 10 minutes. Crush the remaining 2 cloves of garlic. In a small bowl, combine the garlic with the remainder of the olive oil, the basil, and the rosemary. Lightly oil 2 large baking sheets. Place one piece of dough onto each sheet and, using floured fingers, press the dough evenly over the bottom (the dough may not completely cover the bottom).

4. With a pastry brush, liberally brush the surface of each focaccia with the garlic oil. Bake the focaccia in the bottom third of a preheated 400°F oven for 18 to 24 minutes, until golden brown. Transfer to wire racks and allow to cool slightly. Serve warm or at room temperature.

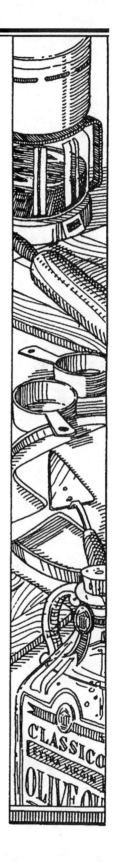

$\mathcal{I}$talian Bread

INGREDIENT	1-POUND LOAF	1^1/2-POUND LOAF
Bread flour	1^1/4 cups	1^1/2 cups
Whole wheat flour	1^1/4 cups	1^1/2 cups
Grated Asiago or Parmesan cheese	3 tablespoons	5 tablespoons
Minced fresh parsley, or dried parsley	2 tablespoons 2 teaspoons	3 tablespoons 1 tablespoon
Minced fresh basil, or dried basil	1 tablespoon 1 teaspoon	1^1/2 tablespoons 1^1/2 teaspoons
Dry milk	1 tablespoon	1^1/2 tablespoons
Minced fresh oregano, or dried oregano	2 teaspoons ^{1}/2 teaspoon	1 tablespoon 1 teaspoon
Garlic, crushed	1 clove	2 cloves
Sea salt	1 teaspoon	1^1/2 teaspoons
Water	1 cup	1^1/4 cups
Olive oil	3 tablespoons	4 tablespoons
Honey	1 tablespoon	1^1/2 tablespoons
Active dry yeast	1 package	4 teaspoons

This is definitely not the Italian bread you find in supermarkets but rather a much more flavorful version, easily prepared in your breadmaker.

1. Fit the kneading blade firmly on the shaft in the bread pan. Carefully measure the dry ingredients and transfer to the pan. Add the liquid ingredients and the yeast. Place the bread pan inside the machine and close the lid.

2. Program the breadmaker for the whole wheat mode. The unit will begin its operation.

3. At the end of the baking cycle, remove the bread promptly from the machine, taking care, as the oven surfaces will be very hot. Invert the bread pan onto a wire rack and shake several times to dislodge the bread. Allow to cool completely on the rack before slicing or wrapping for storage.

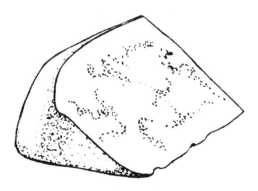

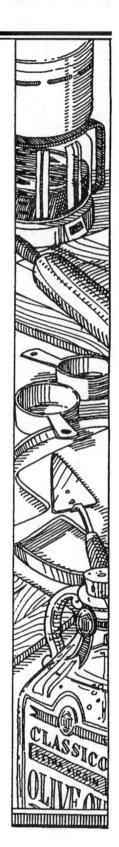

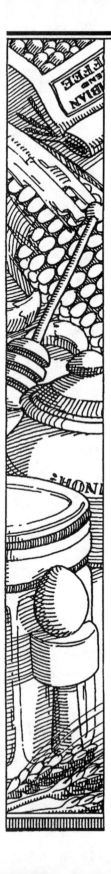

Mustard Curry Bread

INGREDIENT	1-POUND LOAF	1^1/$_2$-POUND LOAF
Bread flour	1^1/$_2$ cups	1^3/$_4$ cups
Whole wheat flour	1 cup	1^1/$_4$ cups
Dry milk	1 tablespoon	1^1/$_2$ tablespoons
VegeBase	1 tablespoon	1^1/$_2$ tablespoons
Curry powder	1 tablespoon	1^1/$_2$ tablespoons
Sea salt	1 teaspoon	1^1/$_2$ teaspoons
Water	1 cup	1^1/$_4$ cups
Dijon-style mustard	2 tablespoons	3 tablespoons
Olive oil	1 tablespoon	2 tablespoons
Honey	1 teaspoon	1 teaspoon
Active dry yeast	2 teaspoons	1 package

The aroma and flavor of this intriguing bread are fantastic and add a real spark to rather plain entrées. You will love the great yellow color, too!

1. Fit the kneading blade firmly on the shaft in the bread pan. Carefully measure the dry ingredients and transfer to the pan. Add the liquid ingredients and the yeast. Place the bread pan inside the machine and close the lid.

2. Program the breadmaker for the whole wheat mode. The unit will begin its operation.

3. At the end of the baking cycle, remove the bread promptly from the machine, taking care, as the oven surfaces will be very hot. Invert the bread pan onto a wire rack and shake several times to dislodge the bread. Allow to cool completely on the rack before slicing or wrapping for storage.

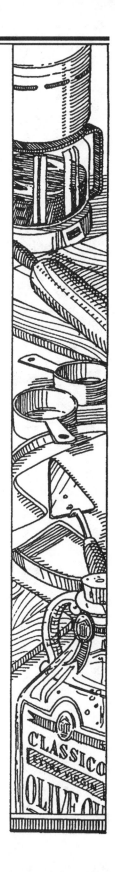

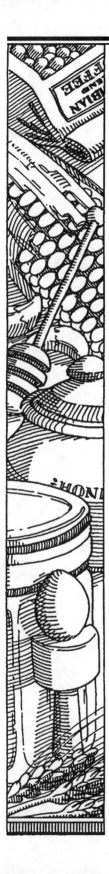

Pita Pockets

INGREDIENT	1-POUND LOAF	1¹/₂-POUND LOAF
Bread flour	2¹/₄ cups	3 cups
Sea salt	1 teaspoon	1¹/₂ teaspoons
Water	⁷/₈ cup	1¹/₄ cups
Olive oil	1 tablespoon	2 tablespoons
Honey	1 teaspoon	1¹/₂ teaspoons
Active dry yeast	2 teaspoons	1 package
Yellow cornmeal	1 tablespoon	2 tablespoons

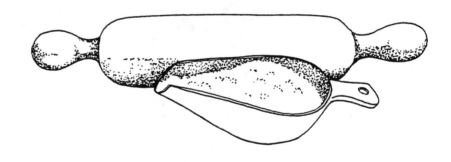

 58

These are pitas made with bread flour, which makes them softer and more likely to balloon than the whole wheat flour pita pockets on the following pages. Try both recipes and see which you prefer.

1. Fit the kneading blade firmly on the shaft in the bread pan. Carefully measure the flour and sea salt, and transfer to the pan. Add the water, olive oil, honey, and yeast. Place the bread pan inside the machine and close the lid.

2. Program the breadmaker for the whole wheat dough mode. The unit will begin its operation.

3. At the end of the rising cycle, turn the dough out onto a lightly floured surface. Cover and let rest 10 minutes. Oil 2 large baking sheets and sprinkle with the cornmeal.

4. Cut the dough into 8 (or 12) equal portions. Flatten each piece of dough with the floured palm of your hand and, using a floured rolling pin, roll each piece into a circle 5 inches in diameter. Arrange on the two baking sheets.

5. In a preheated 475°F oven, place one sheet on the lowest rack and bake for $4^1/2$ minutes. Transfer to the top rack and place the other sheet on the bottom rack. After a second $4^1/2$-minute period, remove the top sheet from the oven, stack the pitas, and wrap them in a dry towel. Wrap a wet towel around the dry one and set aside. Transfer the remaining sheet from the bottom rack to the top one; bake for $4^1/2$ minutes more, then remove from the oven and add the pitas to the towels. Allow the pitas to cool completely in the towels before removing and wrapping for storage. Makes 8 (or 12) pitas.

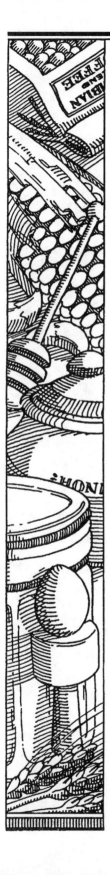

*R*osemary Pita Pockets

INGREDIENT	1-POUND LOAF	1½-POUND LOAF
Whole wheat flour	1½ cups	1¾ cups
Bread flour	½ cup	¾ cup
Gluten flour	½ cup	½ cup
Minced fresh rosemary, or dried rosemary	1 tablespoon 1 teaspoon	2 tablespoons 2 teaspoons
Snipped fresh chives	1 tablespoon	2 tablespoons
Minced fresh basil, or dried basil	2 teaspoons ½ teaspoon	1 tablespoon 1 teaspoon
Sea salt	1 teaspoon	1½ teaspoons
Water	1 cup	1¼ cups
Olive oil	2 tablespoons	3 tablespoons
Active dry yeast	1 package	4 teaspoons
Yellow cornmeal	1 tablespoon	2 tablespoons
Egg, beaten	1 large	1 large

This flavorful version of pita bread includes seasonings that elevate it beyond the sometimes uninteresting loaves you find in markets.

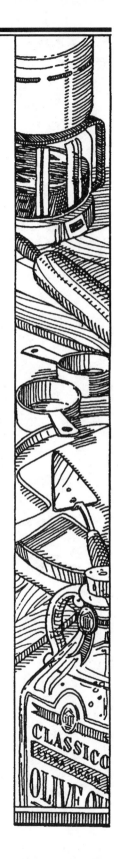

1. Fit the kneading blade firmly on the shaft in the bread pan. Carefully measure the flour and sea salt, and transfer to the pan. Add the water, olive oil, and yeast. Place the bread pan inside the machine and close the lid.

2. Program the breadmaker for the whole wheat dough mode. The unit will begin its operation.

3. At the end of the rising cycle, turn the dough out onto a lightly floured surface. Cover and let rest 10 minutes. Oil 2 large baking sheets and sprinkle with the cornmeal.

4. Cut the dough into 8 (or 12) equal portions. Flatten each piece of dough with the floured palm of your hand and, using a floured rolling pin, roll each piece into a circle 5 inches in diameter. Arrange on the 2 baking sheets, and brush each circle with the beaten egg.

5. In a preheated 475°F oven, place one sheet on the lowest rack and bake for $4^1/2$ minutes. Transfer to the top rack and place the other sheet on the bottom rack. After a second $4^1/2$-minute period, remove the top sheet from the oven, stack the pitas, and wrap them in a dry towel. Wrap a wet towel around the dry one and set aside. Transfer the remaining sheet from the bottom rack to the top one; bake for $4^1/2$ minutes more, then remove from the oven and add the pitas to the towels. Allow the pitas to cool completely in the towels before removing and wrapping for storage. Makes 8 (or 12) pitas.

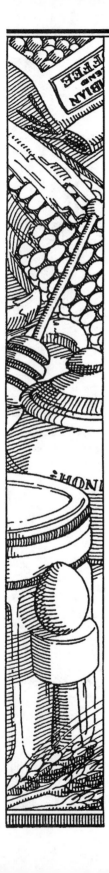

Semolina Bread

INGREDIENT	1-POUND LOAF	1^1/$_2$-POUND LOAF
Whole wheat flour	1^1/$_4$ cups	1^1/$_3$ cups
Bread flour	1 cup	1^1/$_3$ cups
Semolina	^{1}/$_4$ cup	^{1}/$_3$ cup
Grated orange zest	1 tablespoon	2 tablespoons
Dry milk	1 tablespoon	1^1/$_2$ tablespoons
Coarsely ground sesame seeds	1 tablespoon	1^1/$_2$ tablespoons
Date sugar	1 teaspoon	2 teaspoons
Sea salt	1 teaspoon	1^1/$_2$ teaspoons
Water	1 cup	1^1/$_4$ cups
Canola, safflower, or sunflower oil	1 tablespoon	2 tablespoons
Active dry yeast	1 package	4 teaspoons

You will find that this light and airy bread has a gentle, uncompromising taste and makes delightful French toast.

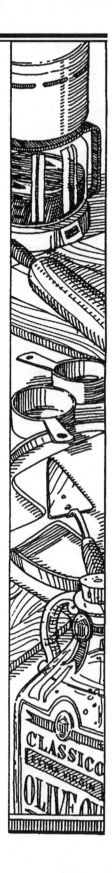

1. Fit the kneading blade firmly on the shaft in the bread pan. Carefully measure the dry ingredients and transfer to the pan. Add the liquid ingredients and the yeast. Place the bread pan inside the machine and close the lid.

2. Program the breadmaker for the whole wheat mode. The unit will begin its operation.

3. At the end of the baking cycle, remove the bread promptly from the machine, taking care, as the oven surfaces will be very hot. Invert the bread pan onto a wire rack and shake several times to dislodge the bread. Allow to cool completely on the rack before slicing or wrapping for storage.

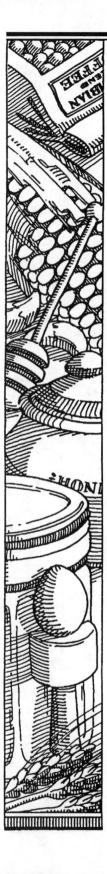

*S*ourdough Coffee Bread

INGREDIENT	1-POUND LOAF	1^1/$_2$-POUND LOAF
Whole wheat flour	1^1/$_2$ cups	1^3/$_4$ cups
Bread flour	^{3}/$_4$ cup	1 cup
Gluten flour	^{1}/$_4$ cup	^{1}/$_4$ cup
Dry milk	1 tablespoon	1^1/$_2$ tablespoons
Sea salt	1 teaspoon	1^1/$_2$ teaspoons
Malt Sourdough Starter (see page 79)	^{1}/$_2$ cup	^{3}/$_4$ cup
Water	^{1}/$_2$ cup	^{1}/$_2$ cup plus 2 tablespoons
Cold coffee	^{1}/$_4$ cup	^{1}/$_4$ cup
Canola, safflower, or sunflower oil	1 tablespoon	2 tablespoons
Honey	1 teaspoon	2 teaspoons
Active dry yeast	1 package	4 teaspoons

Combining the coffee and the Malt Sourdough Starter gives this high and quite light bread a very subtle, arresting flavor.

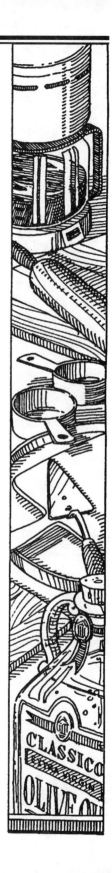

1. Fit the kneading blade firmly on the shaft in the bread pan. Carefully measure the dry ingredients and transfer to the pan. Add the liquid ingredients and the yeast. Place the bread pan inside the machine and close the lid.

2. Program the breadmaker for the whole wheat mode. The unit will begin its operation.

3. At the end of the baking cycle, remove the bread promptly from the machine, taking care, as the oven surfaces will be very hot. Invert the bread pan onto a wire rack and shake several times to dislodge the bread. Allow to cool completely on the rack before slicing or wrapping for storage.

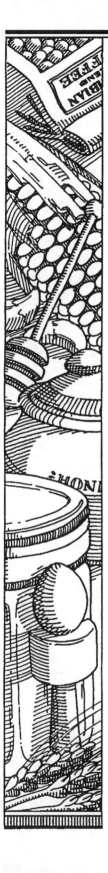

Sun-Dried Tomato and Rosemary Bread

INGREDIENT	1-POUND LOAF	1¹/₂-POUND LOAF
Whole wheat flour	1¹/₄ cups	1¹/₂ cups
Bread flour	1¹/₄ cups	1¹/₂ cups
Minced fresh basil, or dried basil	1 tablespoon 1 teaspoon	2 tablespoons 2 teaspoons
Minced fresh rosemary, or dried rosemary	1 tablespoon 1 teaspoon	2 tablespoons 1¹/₂ teaspoons
Sea salt	1 teaspoon	1¹/₂ teaspoons
Garlic, crushed	1 clove	2 cloves
Sun-dried tomatoes, drained and minced	2	3
Water	1 cup	1¹/₄ cups
Olive oil	1 tablespoon	2 tablespoons
Honey	1 teaspoon	2 teaspoons
Active dry yeast	1 package	4 teaspoons

This rose-colored bread has a very prominent flavor and is ideal served with robust dishes.

1. Fit the kneading blade firmly on the shaft in the bread pan. Carefully measure the dry ingredients and transfer to the pan. Add the liquid ingredients and the yeast. Place the bread pan inside the machine and close the lid.

2. Program the breadmaker for the whole wheat mode. The unit will begin its operation.

3. At the end of the baking cycle, remove the bread promptly from the machine, taking care, as the oven surfaces will be very hot. Invert the bread pan onto a wire rack and shake several times to dislodge the bread. Allow to cool completely on the rack before slicing or wrapping for storage.

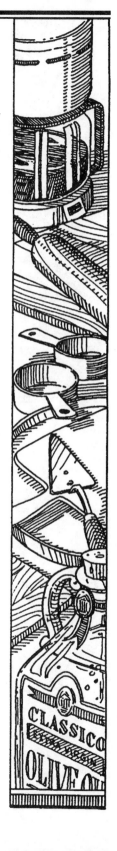

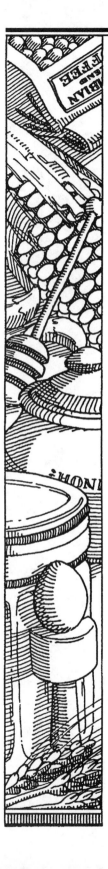

$\mathscr{S}$wedish Limpa Bread

INGREDIENT	1-POUND LOAF	1¹/₂-POUND LOAF
Bread flour	1³/₄ cups	2 cups
Whole rye flour	³/₄ cup	1 cup
Date sugar	2 tablespoons	3 tablespoons
Dry milk	1 tablespoon	1¹/₂ tablespoons
Caraway seeds	1 tablespoon	4 teaspoons
Sea salt	1 teaspoon	1¹/₂ teaspoons
Water	1 cup	1¹/₄ cups
Canola, safflower, or sunflower oil	1 tablespoon	2 tablespoons
Active dry yeast	2 teaspoons	1 package

The bread flour creates a very high and light bread, and the caraway gives it a decidedly Scandinavian flavor.

1. Fit the kneading blade firmly on the shaft in the bread pan. Carefully measure the dry ingredients and transfer to the pan. Add the liquid ingredients and the yeast. Place the bread pan inside the machine and close the lid.

2. Program the breadmaker for the whole wheat mode. The unit will begin its operation.

3. At the end of the baking cycle, remove the bread promptly from the machine, taking care, as the oven surfaces will be very hot. Invert the bread pan onto a wire rack and shake several times to dislodge the bread. Allow to cool completely on the rack before slicing or wrapping for storage.

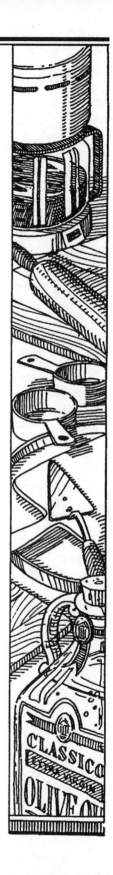

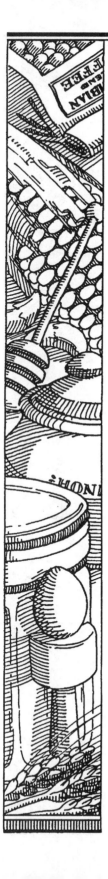

*S*weet Portuguese Wheat Bread

INGREDIENT	1-POUND LOAF	1½-POUND LOAF
Whole wheat flour	1¼ cups	1½ cups
Bread flour	1¼ cups	1½ cups
Dry milk	1 tablespoon	2 tablespoons
Sea salt	1 teaspoon	1½ teaspoons
Water	⅞ cup	1 cup plus 2 tablespoons
Canola, safflower, or sunflower oil	3 tablespoons	¼ cup
Honey	3 tablespoons	¼ cup
Active dry yeast	1 package	4 teaspoons
Egg, beaten	1 large	1 large
Date sugar	2 tablespoons	3 tablespoons

While this bread can be baked in the breadmaker, I prefer removing the dough after it has risen and baking it in a round cake pan. This allows me to slash and glaze the top, which increases its visual appeal.

1. Fit the kneading blade firmly on the shaft in the bread pan. Carefully measure the flours, dry milk, and salt, and transfer to the pan. Add the water, oil, honey, and yeast. Place the bread pan inside the machine and close the lid.

2. Program the breadmaker for the whole wheat dough mode. The unit will begin its operation.

3. At the end of the rising cycle, turn the dough out onto a floured board. Lightly oil a 9-inch round cake pan. With floured hands, form the dough into a large ball. Flatten the ball slightly and transfer to the prepared pan. Cover the pan and let the dough rise for 30 minutes.

4. With a sharp knife, cut a deep X in the top of the dough. Lightly brush the top with the beaten egg and sprinkle liberally with the date sugar. Bake the bread in a preheated 450°F oven for 10 minutes. Reduce the temperature to 350°F and bake 35 to 40 minutes, until the bread is golden brown. Transfer to a wire rack and allow to cool before slicing or wrapping for storage.

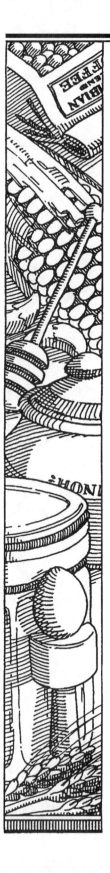

100% *Whole Wheat Pizza Dough*

INGREDIENT	1-POUND LOAF	1$\frac{1}{2}$-POUND LOAF
Whole wheat flour	2$\frac{1}{4}$ cups	2$\frac{2}{3}$ cups
Gluten flour	$\frac{1}{4}$ cup	$\frac{1}{3}$ cup
Date sugar	1 teaspoon	1$\frac{1}{2}$ teaspoons
Sea salt	1 teaspoon	1$\frac{1}{2}$ teaspoons
Water	1 cup	1$\frac{1}{4}$ cups
Olive oil	2 tablespoons	3 tablespoons
Active dry yeast	1 package	4 teaspoons
Cornmeal	1 teaspoon	1$\frac{1}{2}$ teaspoons

Incredibly simple when made in a breadmaker, this recipe yields one 12-inch (or, if you have a larger machine, a 15-inch) pizza crust.

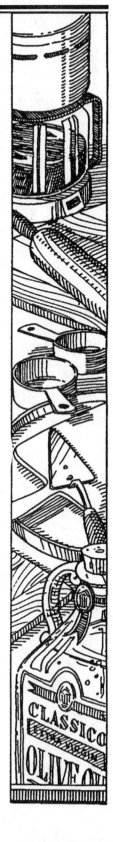

1. Fit the kneading blade firmly on the shaft in the bread pan. Carefully measure the flours, salt, and sugar, and transfer to the pan. Add the water, oil, and yeast. Place the bread pan inside the machine and close the lid.

2. Program the breadmaker for the whole wheat dough mode. The unit will begin its operation.

3. At the end of the rising cycle, turn the dough out onto a lightly floured surface. Cover and let rest for 10 minutes.

4. Lightly oil a 12-inch (or 15-inch) pizza pan and sprinkle with the cornmeal. With floured hands, gently stretch the dough into a 12-inch (or 15-inch) circle and place in the prepared pan. Continue stretching until the dough covers the entire surface of the pan. Push the dough against the rim of the pan to make an edge, then top the dough with your choice of pizza fillings.

5. Bake the pizza on the bottom rack of a preheated 400°F oven for 20 to 25 minutes, until the crust is golden and the filling is melted and bubbly. Serve hot.

Half-and-Half Pizza Dough

INGREDIENT	1-POUND LOAF	1^1/$_2$-POUND LOAF
Bread flour	1^1/$_4$ cups	1^1/$_2$ cups
Whole wheat flour	1^1/$_4$ cups	1^1/$_2$ cups
Sea salt	1 teaspoon	1^1/$_2$ teaspoons
Date sugar	1 teaspoon	1^1/$_2$ teaspoons
Water	1 cup	1^1/$_4$ cups
Olive oil	2 tablespoons	3 tablespoons
Active dry yeast	1 package	4 teaspoons
Cornmeal	1 teaspoon	1^1/$_2$ teaspoons

Using half bread flour and half whole wheat flour results in a lighter, less chewy pizza dough. The quantities for the 1-pound loaf make a 12-inch pizza; the quantities for the 1¹/2-pound loaf make a 15-inch pizza.

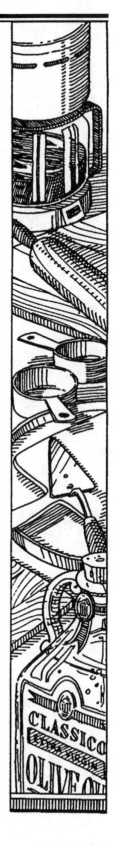

1. Fit the kneading blade firmly on the shaft in the bread pan. Carefully measure the flours, date sugar, and salt, and transfer to the pan. Add the water, oil, and yeast. Place the bread pan inside the machine and close the lid.

2. Program the breadmaker for the whole wheat dough mode. The unit will begin its operation.

3. At the end of the rising cycle, turn the dough out onto a lightly floured surface. Cover and let rest for 10 minutes.

4. Lightly oil a 12-inch (or 15-inch) pizza pan and sprinkle with the cornmeal. With floured hands, gently stretch the dough into a 12-inch (or 15-inch) circle and place in the prepared pan. Continue stretching until the dough covers the entire surface of the pan. Push the dough against the rim of the pan to make an edge, then top the dough with your choice of pizza fillings.

5. Bake the pizza on the bottom rack of a preheated 400°F oven for 20 to 25 minutes, until the crust is golden and the filling is melted and bubbly. Serve hot.

$\mathcal{S}$oft Pretzels

INGREDIENT	1-POUND LOAF	1¹/₂-POUND LOAF
Whole wheat flour	1¹/₂ cups	1³/₄ cups
Bread flour	1 cup	1¹/₄ cups
Sea salt	1 teaspoon	1¹/₂ teaspoons
Water	1 quart plus 1 cup	1 quart plus 1¹/₄ cups
Honey	1 teaspoon	2 teaspoons
Active dry yeast	1 package	4 teaspoons
Baking soda	3 tablespoons	¹/₄ cup
Date sugar	1 tablespoon	1¹/₂ tablespoons
Coarse sea salt	1 tablespoon	2 tablespoons

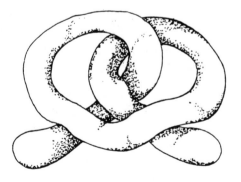

Ever since my years in New York, I have had a special place in my heart for big, soft, hot pretzels bought from street corner vendors. This is my version—a snap to make in a breadmaker.

1. Fit the kneading blade firmly on the shaft in the bread pan. Carefully measure the flours and salt, and add to the pan. Add the 1 cup (or 1¼ cups) of water, the honey, and the yeast. Place the bread pan inside the machine and close the lid.

2. Program the breadmaker for the whole wheat dough mode. The unit will begin its operation.

3. At the end of the rising cycle, turn the dough out onto a lightly floured surface. Cover and let it rest for 10 minutes. Cut the dough into 8 (or 12) equal pieces. With floured hands, roll each piece into a rope about 16 inches long with tapered ends. Form each into a pretzel shape and place on a lightly floured board. Cover and let rise for 30 minutes.

4. In a very large, deep skillet, combine the 1 quart of water, the baking soda, and the sugar, and bring to a simmer. Slide 3 pretzels at a time into the simmering water and cook for 20 seconds. Flip over gently with a spatula and cook for 20 seconds more. Remove with a slotted spoon, allowing the water to drain back into the skillet, and place on a clean cloth towel. Repeat until all the pretzels are cooked.

5. Cover a baking sheet with parchment paper and arrange the pretzels on the sheet, rounded tops up. Sprinkle lightly with the coarse salt. Bake the pretzels in a preheated 425°F oven for 12 to 14 minutes, until golden. Remove from the baking sheet and cool. Makes 8 (or 12) pretzels.

Sourdough Starter

Yield: 1¹/₂ cups   *Time: 3 to 5 days*

This sourdough starter works well with almost any bread-flour recipe and is easily stored in the refrigerator.

INGREDIENT	AMOUNT
Bread flour	1¹/₂ cups
Water, at room temperature	1¹/₂ cups
Dry milk	¹/₂ teaspoon
Active dry yeast	¹/₈ teaspoon

1. In a glass bowl, combine all the ingredients and stir well. Cover tightly with plastic wrap and let stand at room temperature for 3 to 5 days, stirring twice a day, until fermented and sour-smelling.

2. Store the starter in the refrigerator until needed. Let it come to room temperature before using.

3. To replenish the starter, replace what you removed with an equal amount of flour and water. Stir well and refrigerate again.

*M*alt Sourdough Starter

Yield: 1¹/₂ cups   *Time: 3 days*

This starter becomes quite sour because of the mashed potatoes and lends a very noticeable flavor to breads.

INGREDIENT	AMOUNT
Malt liquor	1 can (12 ounces)
Mashed potatoes	1 cup
Honey	1¹/₂ tablespoons
Sea salt	1 teaspoon
Active dry yeast	¹/₂ teaspoon

1. In a medium bowl, combine all the ingredients and stir well. Cover tightly with plastic wrap and let stand at room temperature for 3 days, stirring twice a day, until fermented and sour-smelling.

2. Store the starter in the refrigerator until needed. Let it come to room temperature before using.

CHAPTER 3

RYE, PUMPERNICKEL, & OTHER DARK BREADS

R ye bread is a traditional bread that comes in many textures, flavors, sizes, and shapes. Although rye is grown all over the world, the great classic rye breads come from eastern and northern Europe.

If you're used to wheat flour, you will find some interesting differences when you bake with rye flour. Rye and wheat flour have a great deal in common nutritionally, but they differ not only in flavor but also in the final texture of the bread. When you include rye flour in a dough, it adds a denseness, and the bread is darker and has more moisture. When you work rye dough with your hands, you will find it stiffer and more difficult to handle, a problem easily solved by using an automatic breadmaker.

Rye flours come in so many varieties of grinds and colors that it is difficult to know what to buy. Generally, the commercial rye

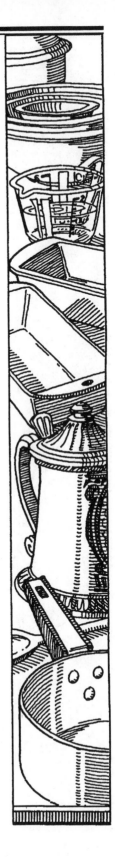

flour available in supermarkets is, unfortunately, a "white" rye flour that is very refined. Before you succumb to buying one of these ryes, try to find a whole rye flour that has kept much of its germ and bran. Your local natural foods store may be a good source of this ingredient.

Many of the recipes in this section are sourdough breads. This is because rye lends itself to the process of fermentation, which imparts a distinctive tang to the bread. Also included here are pumpernickel and other dark breads, which either come from or are reminiscent of Scandinavia and eastern Europe. I find these breads to be the most satisfying of all the breads, largely, I am sure, because they were the breads of my childhood. Hearty, dense, and dark, they do not just complement a meal, but demand that their presence be noticed.

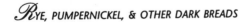

Beer Rye

INGREDIENT	1-POUND LOAF	1¹/2-POUND LOAF
Whole wheat flour	1¹/2 cups	1³/4 cups
Whole rye flour	³/4 cup	1 cup
Snipped fresh dill, or dried dillweed	3 tablespoons 1 tablespoon	¹/4 cup 1¹/2 tablespoons
Yellow cornmeal	2 tablespoons	2 tablespoons
Wheat germ	2 tablespoons	2 tablespoons
Dry milk	1 tablespoon	2 tablespoons
Caraway seeds	1 tablespoon	1¹/2 tablespoons
Sea salt	1 teaspoon	1¹/2 teaspoons
Beer, flat and at room temperature	1 cup	1¹/4 cups
Canola, safflower, or sunflower oil	1 tablespoon	2 tablespoons
Active dry yeast	1 package	4 teaspoons

This light rye is a terrific sandwich bread and will not overwhelm the ingredients you nestle between its slices.

1. Fit the kneading blade firmly on the shaft in the bread pan. Carefully measure the dry ingredients and transfer to the pan. Add the liquid ingredients and the yeast. Place the bread pan inside the machine and close the lid.

2. Program the breadmaker for the whole wheat mode. The unit will begin its operation.

3. At the end of the baking cycle, remove the bread promptly from the machine, taking care, as the oven surfaces will be very hot. Invert the bread pan onto a wire rack and shake several times to dislodge the bread. Allow to cool completely on the rack before slicing or wrapping for storage.

*B*oston Brown Bread

INGREDIENT	1-POUND LOAF	1 1/2-POUND LOAF
Whole rye flour	1 cup	1 1/4 cups
Whole wheat flour	1 cup	1 1/4 cups
Gluten flour	1/4 cup	1/4 cup
Yellow cornmeal	1/4 cup	1/4 cup
Cocoa or carob powder	2 tablespoons	3 tablespoons
Baking soda	1/4 teaspoon	1/2 teaspoon
Buttermilk	7/8 cup	1 cup plus 3 tablespoons
Molasses	1/4 cup	1/3 cup
Canola, safflower, or sunflower oil	1 tablespoon	3 tablespoons
Active dry yeast	1 package	4 teaspoons
Dried currants	1/4 cup	1/3 cup

Do not worry when this bread does not rise much. It has a delightful, intense flavor and is best sliced very thin and served with soft cream cheese. Be sure not to add the currants until the start of the kneading cycle.

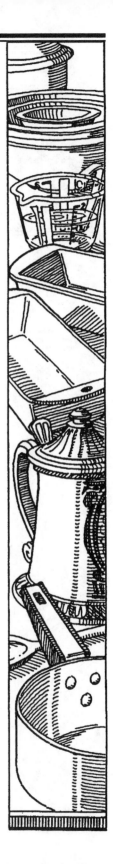

1. Fit the kneading blade firmly on the shaft in the bread pan. Carefully measure the flours, cornmeal, cocoa, and baking soda, and transfer to the pan. Add the liquid ingredients and the yeast. Place the bread pan inside the machine and close the lid.

2. Program the breadmaker for the whole wheat mode. The unit will begin its operation.

3. At the end of the mixing cycle and just before the kneading cycle begins, add the currants to the dough.

4. At the end of the baking cycle, remove the bread promptly from the machine, taking care, as the oven surfaces will be very hot. Invert the bread pan onto a wire rack and shake several times to dislodge the bread. Allow to cool completely on the rack before slicing or wrapping for storage. Serve with cream cheese.

$\mathcal{D}$ark Rye Bread

INGREDIENT	1-POUND LOAF	1^1/$_2$-POUND LOAF
Whole wheat flour	1^3/4 cups	2 cups
Whole rye flour	^{1}/2 cup	^{1}/2 cup
Gluten flour	^{1}/4 cup	^{1}/2 cup
Cocoa or carob powder	1 tablespoon	2 tablespoons
Caraway seeds	1 teaspoon	2 teaspoons
Sea salt	1 teaspoon	1^1/2 teaspoons
Water	^{2}/3 cup	^{3}/4 cup
Plain nonfat yogurt	^{1}/3 cup	^{1}/2 cup
Canola, safflower, or sunflower oil	1 tablespoon	2 tablespoons
Apple cider vinegar	1 tablespoon	1 tablespoon
Honey	1 teaspoon	1^1/2 teaspoons
Active dry yeast	1 package	4 teaspoons

The cocoa gives this substantial bread its rich brown color and a hint of flavor.

1. Fit the kneading blade firmly on the shaft in the bread pan. Carefully measure the dry ingredients and transfer to the pan. Add the liquid ingredients and the yeast. Place the bread pan inside the machine and close the lid.

2. Program the breadmaker for the whole wheat mode. The unit will begin its operation.

3. At the end of the baking cycle, remove the bread promptly from the machine, taking care, as the oven surfaces will be very hot. Invert the bread pan onto a wire rack and shake several times to dislodge the bread. Allow to cool completely on the rack before slicing or wrapping for storage.

*H*ops Rye Bread

INGREDIENT	1-POUND LOAF	1 1/2-POUND LOAF
Whole wheat flour	1 1/2 cups	1 2/3 cups
Whole rye flour	3/4 cup	1 cup
Gluten flour	1/4 cup	1/3 cup
Caraway seeds	2 tablespoons	1 tablespoon
Grated orange zest	1 teaspoon	2 teaspoons
Sea salt	1 teaspoon	1 1/2 teaspoons
Malt Sourdough Starter (see page 79)	1 cup	1 1/4 cups
Water	7 tablespoons	1 cup plus 2 tablespoons
Canola, safflower, or sunflower oil	1 tablespoon	2 tablespoons
Honey	1 teaspoon	1 teaspoon
Active dry yeast	1 package	4 teaspoons

*T*HE BREAD MACHINE GOURMET

Top: 100% Whole Wheat Pizza Dough (page72)
Topped With Sauce and Vegetables
Bottom: Half-and-Half Pizza Dough (page 74)
Topped With Sauce and Cheese

Top Left: Hops Rye Bread (page 88)
Top Right: Dark Rye Bread (page 86)
Bottom: Pumpernickel (page 94)

*An enticing sour rye flavor graces this
nutritionally rich bread.*

1. Fit the kneading blade firmly
on the shaft in the bread pan. Carefully measure the dry
ingredients and transfer to the pan. Add the liquid ingredients
and the yeast. Place the bread pan inside the machine and close
the lid.

2. Program the breadmaker for
the whole wheat mode. The unit will begin its operation.

3. At the end of the baking cycle,
remove the bread promptly from the machine, taking care, as the
oven surfaces will be very hot. Invert the bread pan onto a wire
rack and shake several times to dislodge the bread. Allow to cool
completely on the rack before slicing or wrapping for storage.

Norwegian Rye Bread

INGREDIENT	1-POUND LOAF	1½-POUND LOAF
Bread flour	1½ cups	1⅔ cups
Whole rye flour	¾ cup	1 cup
Graham flour	¼ cup	⅓ cup
Coarsely ground anise seeds	1 tablespoon	1½ tablespoons
Sea salt	1 teaspoon	1½ teaspoons
Buttermilk	⅜ cup	½ cup
Water	½ cup	½ cup plus 2 tablespoons
Molasses	¼ cup	⅓ cup
Canola, safflower, or sunflower oil	2 tablespoons	3 tablespoons
Active dry yeast	1 package	4 teaspoons

THE BREAD MACHINE GOURMET

This is an authentic version of one of the most savory breads the Norwegians claim as their own.

1. Fit the kneading blade firmly on the shaft in the bread pan. Carefully measure the dry ingredients and transfer to the pan. Add the liquid ingredients and the yeast. Place the bread pan inside the machine and close the lid.

2. Program the breadmaker for the whole wheat mode. The unit will begin its operation.

3. At the end of the baking cycle, remove the bread promptly from the machine, taking care, as the oven surfaces will be very hot. Invert the bread pan onto a wire rack and shake several times to dislodge the bread. Allow to cool completely on the rack before slicing or wrapping for storage.

Onion Sourdough Rye

INGREDIENT	1-POUND LOAF	1^1/2-POUND LOAF
Minced sweet yellow onion	^{1}/2 cup (about 1 small)	^{2}/3 cup (about 1 small)
Sourdough Rye Starter (see page 104)	^{1}/2 cup	^{2}/3 cup
Bread flour	2 cups	2^1/3 cups
Whole rye flour	^{1}/2 cup	^{2}/3 cup
Ground caraway seeds	2 tablespoons	3 tablespoons
Dry milk	1 tablespoon	1^1/2 tablespoons
Sea salt	1 teaspoon	1^1/2 teaspoons
Date sugar	^{1}/2 teaspoon	1 teaspoon
Water	^{1}/2 cup	^{2}/3 cup
Plain nonfat yogurt	^{1}/4 cup	5 tablespoons
Canola, safflower, or sunflower oil	1 tablespoon	2 tablespoons
Active dry yeast	2 teaspoons	1 package

*Lots of nutrition in this delicious bread—
lots of flavor, too.*

1. The day before you wish to make this bread, place the onions in a small bowl with the starter. Cover the bowl and leave at room temperature for 12 hours.

2. Fit the kneading blade firmly on the shaft in the bread pan. Carefully measure the dry ingredients and transfer to the pan. Add the onions and starter, water, yogurt, oil, and yeast. Place the bread pan inside the machine and close the lid.

3. Program the breadmaker for the whole wheat mode. The unit will begin its operation.

4. At the end of the baking cycle, remove the bread promptly from the machine, taking care, as the oven surfaces will be very hot. Invert the bread pan onto a wire rack and shake several times to dislodge the bread. Allow to cool completely on the rack before slicing or wrapping for storage.

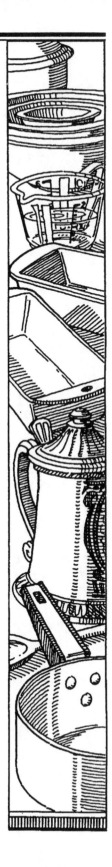

$\mathcal{P}$umpernickel

INGREDIENT	1-POUND LOAF	1¹/₂-POUND LOAF
Date sugar	¹/₃ cup	¹/₄ cup
Water	1 cup plus 2 tablespoons	1¹/₄ cups plus 2 tablespoons
Whole rye flour	1 cup	1¹/₃ cups
Whole wheat flour	¹/₂ cup	²/₃ cup
Bread flour	¹/₂ cup	¹/₂ cup
Gluten flour	¹/₂ cup	¹/₂ cup
Cocoa or carob powder	1 tablespoon	2 tablespoons
Sea salt	1 teaspoon	1¹/₂ teaspoons
Canola, safflower, or sunflower oil	1 tablespoon	2 tablespoons
Active dry yeast	1 package	4 teaspoons

Dark, intense, scrumptious. A true German bread that gets its deep color from caramel.

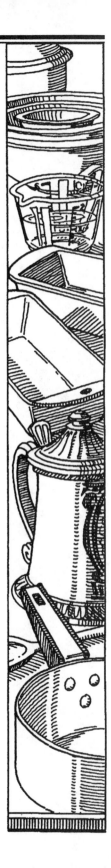

1. In a small pot, heat the date sugar over moderate heat, stirring until it becomes medium-dark brown and frothy. Bring $1/4$ cup of water to a boil and add to the sugar, averting your face as you pour; stir well. Set aside to cool.

2. Fit the kneading blade firmly on the shaft in the bread pan. Carefully measure the dry ingredients and transfer to the pan. Add the cooled caramel, the remainder of the water, the oil, and yeast. Place the bread pan inside the machine and close the lid.

3. Program the breadmaker for the whole wheat mode. The unit will begin its operation.

4. At the end of the baking cycle, remove the bread promptly from the machine, taking care, as the oven surfaces will be very hot. Invert the bread pan onto a wire rack and shake several times to dislodge the bread. Allow to cool completely on the rack before slicing or wrapping for storage.

Pumpernickel Prune Bread

INGREDIENT	1-POUND LOAF	1^1/$_2$-POUND LOAF
Whole wheat flour	1^1/$_2$ cups	1^2/$_3$ cups
Whole rye flour	^{1}/$_2$ cup	^{2}/$_3$ cup
Buckwheat flour	^{1}/$_4$ cup	^{1}/$_3$ cup
Rolled oats	^{1}/$_4$ cup	^{1}/$_3$ cup
Poppy seeds	1 tablespoon	2 tablespoons
Sea salt	1 teaspoon	1^1/$_2$ teaspoons
Water	^{7}/$_8$ cup	1 cup plus 2 tablespoons
Molasses	2 tablespoons	3 tablespoons
Canola, safflower, or sunflower oil	1 tablespoon	2 tablespoons
Active dry yeast	1 package	4 teaspoons
Minced pitted prunes	^{1}/$_2$ cup	^{2}/$_3$ cup

Do not be surprised if this does not rise as high as other breads. It is very dense with a savory flavor, and is best thinly sliced and served with a tangy cheese.

1. Fit the kneading blade firmly on the shaft in the bread pan. Carefully measure the flours, oats, seeds, and salt, and transfer to the pan. Add the liquid ingredients and the yeast. Place the bread pan inside the machine and close the lid.

2. Program the breadmaker for the whole wheat mode. The unit will begin its operation.

3. At the end of the mixing cycle and just before the kneading cycle begins, add the minced prunes to the dough.

4. At the end of the baking cycle, remove the bread promptly from the machine, taking care, as the oven surfaces will be very hot. Invert the bread pan onto a wire rack and shake several times to dislodge the bread. Allow to cool completely on the rack before slicing or wrapping for storage.

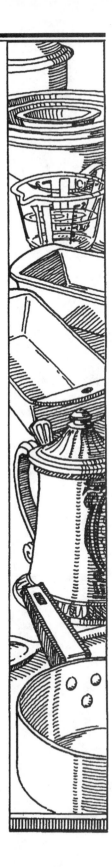

$\mathscr{S}$our Beer Rye

INGREDIENT	1-POUND LOAF	1^{1}/2-POUND LOAF
Beer, flat and at room temperature	3/4 cup	1 cup
Apple cider vinegar	1/4 cup	1/4 cup
Bread flour	1 cup	1^{1}/4 cups
Whole rye flour	3/4 cup	1 cup
Whole wheat flour	1/2 cup	1/2 cup
Gluten flour	1/4 cup	1/4 cup
Snipped fresh dill, or dried dillweed	2 teaspoons 1/2 teaspoon	1 tablespoon 1 teaspoon
Sea salt	1 teaspoon	1^{1}/2 teaspoons
Caraway seeds	1 teaspoon	2 teaspoons
Canola, safflower, or sunflower oil	1 tablespoon	2 tablespoons
Honey	1 tablespoon	1 tablespoon
Active dry yeast	1 package	4 teaspoons

The distinctly sour taste of this bread does not come from a sourdough starter, but from combining cider vinegar with beer. It is a very light, delectable bread.

1. In a small bowl, combine the beer and the vinegar and set aside for 10 minutes.

2. Fit the kneading blade firmly on the shaft in the bread pan. Carefully measure the dry ingredients and transfer to the pan. Add the liquid ingredients, including the beer-and-vinegar mixture, and the yeast. Place the bread pan inside the machine and close the lid.

3. Program the breadmaker for the whole wheat mode. The unit will begin its operation.

4. At the end of the baking cycle, remove the bread promptly from the machine, taking care, as the oven surfaces will be very hot. Invert the bread pan onto a wire rack and shake several times to dislodge the bread. Allow to cool completely on the rack before slicing or wrapping for storage.

Swedish Beer Rye

INGREDIENT	1-POUND LOAF	1¹/₂-POUND LOAF
Beer, flat and at room temperature	$^7/_8$ cup	1$^1/_4$ cups
Caraway seeds	2 teaspoons	1 tablespoon
Whole rye flour	1 cup	1$^1/_4$ cups
Bread flour	$^3/_4$ cup	1 cup
Whole wheat flour	$^1/_2$ cup	$^1/_2$ cup
Gluten flour	$^1/_4$ cup	$^1/_4$ cup
Snipped fresh thyme, or dried thyme	2 teaspoons / $^1/_2$ teaspoon	1 tablespoon / 1 teaspoon
Sea salt	1 teaspoon	1$^1/_2$ teaspoons
Soy margarine	3 tablespoons	4 tablespoons
Molasses	2 tablespoons	3 tablespoons
Active dry yeast	1 package	4 teaspoons

Soaking the caraway seeds in beer for eight hours allows time for the beer to go flat and the essence of the caraway to permeate the liquid.

1. In a small bowl, combine the beer and seeds and set aside at room temperature for 8 hours.

2. Fit the kneading blade firmly on the shaft in the bread pan. Carefully measure the dry ingredients and transfer to the pan. Add the beer and seeds, margarine, molasses, and yeast. Place the bread pan inside the machine and close the lid.

3. Program the breadmaker for the whole wheat mode. The unit will begin its operation.

4. At the end of the baking cycle, remove the bread promptly from the machine, taking care, as the oven surfaces will be very hot. Invert the bread pan onto a wire rack and shake several times to dislodge the bread. Allow to cool completely on the rack before slicing or wrapping for storage.

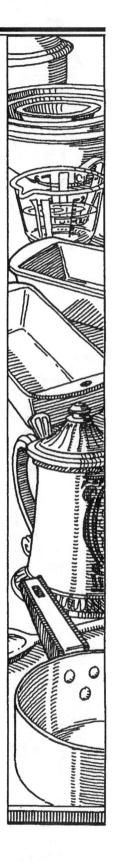

$\mathcal{S}$tout Bread

INGREDIENT	1-POUND LOAF	1$^{1}/_{2}$-POUND LOAF
Whole wheat flour	1$^{1}/_{4}$ cups	1$^{1}/_{2}$ cups
Whole rye flour	1 cup	1$^{1}/_{4}$ cups
Gluten flour	$^{1}/_{4}$ cup	$^{1}/_{4}$ cup
Cocoa or carob powder	2 tablespoons	3 tablespoons
Coarsely ground fennel seeds	2 tablespoons	3 tablespoons
Grated orange zest	1 tablespoon	1$^{1}/_{2}$ tablespoons
Sea salt	1 teaspoon	1$^{1}/_{2}$ teaspoons
Stout or dark beer, flat and at room temperature	$^{5}/_{8}$ cup	$^{7}/_{8}$ cup
Plain nonfat yogurt	6 tablespoons	$^{1}/_{2}$ cup
Molasses	$^{1}/_{4}$ cup	$^{1}/_{3}$ cup
Soy margarine	3 tablespoons	$^{1}/_{4}$ cup
Active dry yeast	1 package	4 teaspoons

 $\mathcal{T}$HE BREAD MACHINE GOURMET

This bread announces its presence with authority and a very distinctive aroma. It is particularly nice when served with a lusty entrée.

1. Fit the kneading blade firmly on the shaft in the bread pan. Carefully measure the dry ingredients and transfer to the pan. Add the liquid ingredients and the yeast. Place the bread pan inside the machine and close the lid.

2. Program the breadmaker for the whole wheat mode. The unit will begin its operation.

3. At the end of the baking cycle, remove the bread promptly from the machine, taking care, as the oven surfaces will be very hot. Invert the bread pan onto a wire rack and shake several times to dislodge the bread. Allow to cool completely on the rack before slicing or wrapping for storage.

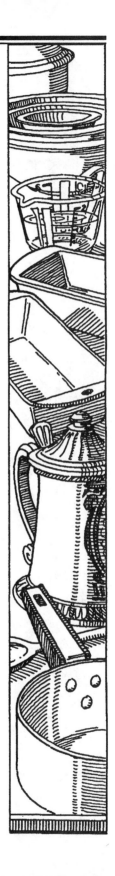

*R*YE, PUMPERNICKEL, & OTHER DARK BREADS   *103*

$\mathcal{S}$ourdough Rye Starter

Yield: 1¹/₂ cups   *Time: 3 to 5 days*

**This sourdough starter can be used interchangeably
with any other starter in this book. It stores
easily in the refrigerator**

INGREDIENT	AMOUNT
Whole rye flour	1¹/₂ cups
Water, at room temperature	1¹/₂ cups
Dry milk	¹/₂ teaspoon
Active dry yeast	¹/₈ teaspoon

1. In a glass bowl, combine the
flour, water, dry milk, and yeast, and stir well. Cover tightly and
let stand at room temperature for 3 to 5 days, stirring twice a day.

---

2. Store the starter in the
refrigerator until needed. Let it come to room temperature before
using.

---

3. To replenish the starter,
replace what starter you remove with equal amounts of flour and
water. Stir well and refrigerate.

CHAPTER 4

BEAN & RICE BREADS

read is a wonderfully nutritious food in itself, yet I constantly search for ways to increase its healthful qualities. Adding beans or rice to a bread dough accomplishes just that. Beans elevate the protein of bread and add a host of intriguing flavors and textures, too. When you eat a bread from this chapter, it will not be like eating the legume itself. The beans and grains won't be obvious in the texture of the bread, but will be part of the dough, lending an air, rather than a presence, to the loaf.

Not all beans are appropriate in a bread dough, although I would encourage you to experiment once you have mastered these recipes. Many beans do not have the body, flavor, or nutritional value of soybeans, black turtle beans, and chick peas. In this chapter, you will find recipes using these beans, as well as a recipe for a quite savory bread that uses kidney beans. All are delicious and packed with satisfyingly high nutrition. You will find that these breads have an appealing fragrance, taste, and texture that can easily become habit-forming.

Black Bean Bread

INGREDIENT	1-POUND LOAF	1^1/2-POUND LOAF
Whole wheat flour	2 cups	2^1/3 cups
Buckwheat flour	^{1}/4 cup	^{1}/3 cup
Gluten flour	^{1}/4 cup	^{1}/3 cup
Minced fresh cilantro, or dried cilantro	1^1/2 tablespoons 2 teaspoons	2^1/2 tablespoons 2 teaspoons
Grated orange zest	1 tablespoon	2 tablespoons
Curry powder	1 teaspoon	2 teaspoons
Crushed garlic	1 clove	2 cloves
Sea salt	1 teaspoon	1^1/2 teaspoons
Ground cumin seeds	^{1}/2 teaspoon	1 teaspoon
Cayenne pepper	^{1}/4 teaspoon, or to taste	^{1}/2 teaspoon, or to taste
Mashed black beans	^{1}/2 cup	^{2}/3 cup
Water	1 cup	1^1/4 cups
Sesame oil	1 tablespoon	1^1/2 tablespoons
Canola, safflower, or sunflower oil	1 tablespoon	1^1/2 tablespoons
Honey	1 teaspoon	2 teaspoons
Active dry yeast	1 package	4 teaspoons

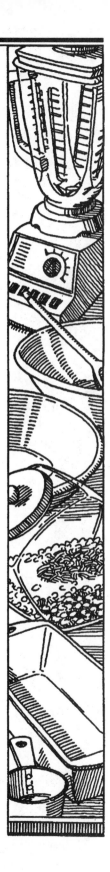

Robust, dark, and very savory, this protein-rich bread is ideal when you are serving a hearty entrée.

1. Fit the kneading blade firmly on the shaft in the bread pan. Carefully measure the dry ingredients and transfer to the pan. Add the beans, liquid ingredients, and yeast. Place the bread pan inside the machine and close the lid.

2. Program the breadmaker for the whole wheat mode. The unit will begin its operation.

3. At the end of the baking cycle, remove the bread promptly from the machine, taking care, as the oven surfaces will be very hot. Invert the bread pan onto a wire rack and shake several times to dislodge the bread. Allow to cool completely on the rack before slicing or wrapping for storage.

$\mathcal{B}$lack Bean and Raisin Bread

INGREDIENT	1-POUND LOAF	1^1/$_2$-POUND LOAF
Cooked, well-drained black beans	1 cup	1^1/$_4$ cups
Water	^{7}/$_8$ cup	1 cup plus 3 tablespoons
Whole wheat flour	2^1/$_4$ cups	2^1/$_2$ cups
Gluten flour	^{1}/$_4$ cup	^{1}/$_2$ cup
Sea salt	1 teaspoon	1^1/$_2$ teaspoons
Molasses	2 tablespoons	3 tablespoons
Canola, safflower, or sunflower oil	1 tablespoon	2 tablespoons
Active dry yeast	1 package	4 teaspoons
Dark raisins	^{1}/$_2$ cup	^{1}/$_2$ cup

$\mathcal{T}$HE BREAD MACHINE GOURMET

This hearty, cakelike bread could easily become a habit. There's a faint sweetness and loads of nutrition in every bite.

1. In a blender or food processor, purée the beans and water until almost smooth.

2. Fit the kneading blade firmly on the shaft in the bread pan. Carefully measure the flours and salt, and transfer to the pan. Add the puréed bean mixture, molasses, oil, and yeast. Place the bread pan inside the machine and close the lid.

3. Program the breadmaker for the whole wheat mode. The unit will begin its operation.

4. At the end of the mixing cycle and just before the kneading cycle begins, add the raisins to the dough.

5. At the end of the baking cycle, remove the bread promptly from the machine, taking care, as the oven surfaces will be very hot. Invert the bread pan onto a wire rack and shake several times to dislodge the bread. Allow to cool completely on the rack before slicing or wrapping for storage.

Brown Rice and Almond Bread

INGREDIENT	1-POUND LOAF	1^1/$_2$-POUND LOAF
Whole wheat flour	2 cups	2^1/$_3$ cups
Cooked brown rice, at room temperature	^{1}/$_2$ cup	^{2}/$_3$ cup
Gluten flour	^{1}/$_4$ cup	^{1}/$_3$ cup
Brown rice flour	^{1}/$_4$ cup	^{1}/$_3$ cup
Toasted and chopped almonds	^{1}/$_4$ cup	^{1}/$_3$ cup
Sea salt	1 teaspoon	1^1/$_2$ teaspoons
Water	1 cup	1^1/$_4$ cups
Canola, safflower, or sunflower oil	1 tablespoon	2 tablespoons
Honey	1 teaspoon	2 teaspoons
Almond extract	^{1}/$_4$ teaspoon	^{1}/$_2$ teaspoon
Active dry yeast	1 package	4 teaspoons

The first time I made this bread I expected that the rice would add an obvious chewiness to the bread, but in fact, the rice is not discernible. What it does add is fiber, good taste, and a full-bodied texture.

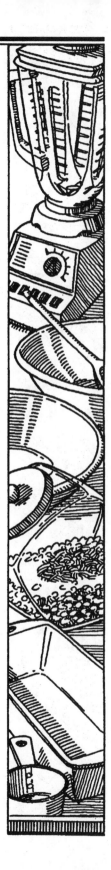

1. Fit the kneading blade firmly on the shaft in the bread pan. Carefully measure the dry ingredients and transfer to the pan. Add the liquid ingredients and yeast. Place the bread pan inside the machine and close the lid.

2. Program the breadmaker for the whole wheat mode. The unit will begin its operation.

3. At the end of the baking cycle, remove the bread promptly from the machine, taking care, as the oven surfaces will be very hot. Invert the bread pan onto a wire rack and shake several times to dislodge the bread. Allow to cool completely on the rack before slicing or wrapping for storage.

Chili Kidney Bean Bread

INGREDIENT	1-POUND LOAF	1^1/2-POUND LOAF
Whole wheat flour	2^1/2 cups	3 cups
Popcorn flour	^{1}/4 cup	^{1}/3 cup
Bouquet garni	1 tablespoon	1^1/2 tablespoons
Chili powder	2 teaspoons	1 tablespoon
Date sugar	1 teaspoon	2 teaspoons
Sea salt	1 teaspoon	1^1/2 teaspoons
Mashed kidney beans	^{3}/4 cup	1 cup
Water	1 cup	1^1/4 cups
Canola, safflower, or sunflower oil	2 tablespoons	2 tablespoons
Active dry yeast	1 package	4 teaspoons

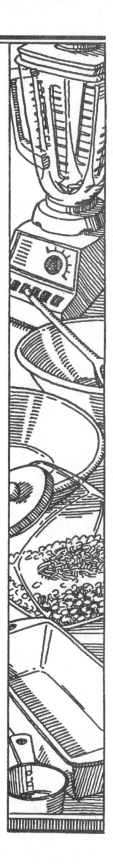

Try sandwiching ripe avocado slices, thin rings of red onion, and a thick slice of Cheddar cheese between pieces of this rich and flavorful aromatic bread.

1. Fit the kneading blade firmly on the shaft in the bread pan. Carefully measure the dry ingredients and transfer to the pan. Add the beans, liquid ingredients, and yeast. Place the bread pan inside the machine and close the lid.

2. Program the breadmaker for the whole wheat mode. The unit will begin its operation.

3. At the end of the baking cycle, remove the bread promptly from the machine, taking care, as the oven surfaces will be very hot. Invert the bread pan onto a wire rack and shake several times to dislodge the bread. Allow to cool completely on the rack before slicing or wrapping for storage.

BEAN & RICE BREADS

Granola Mint Bread

INGREDIENT	1-POUND LOAF	1$\frac{1}{2}$-POUND LOAF
Whole wheat flour	1 cup	1$\frac{1}{4}$ cups
Bread flour	1 cup	1$\frac{1}{4}$ cup
Granola cereal	$\frac{1}{2}$ cup	$\frac{2}{3}$ cup
Cooked brown rice	$\frac{1}{4}$ cup	$\frac{1}{2}$ cup
Sea salt	1 teaspoon	1$\frac{1}{2}$ teaspoons
Water	1 cup	1$\frac{1}{4}$ cups
Canola, safflower, or sunflower oil	2 tablespoons	3 tablespoons
Honey	1 tablespoon	2 tablespoons
Mint extract	$\frac{1}{2}$ teaspoon	$\frac{3}{4}$ teaspoon
Active dry yeast	1 package	4 teaspoons

The granola gives this bread an interesting texture, while the mint extract imparts an intriguing flavor.

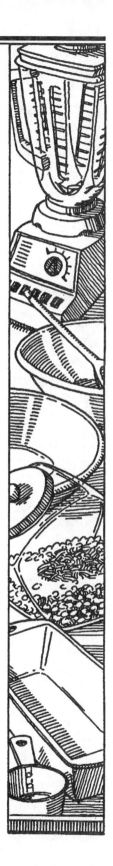

1. Fit the kneading blade firmly on the shaft in the bread pan. Carefully measure the flours, granola, rice, and salt, and transfer to the pan. Add the liquid ingredients and the yeast. Place the bread pan inside the machine and close the lid.

2. Program the breadmaker for the whole wheat mode. The unit will begin its operation.

3. At the end of the baking cycle, remove the bread promptly from the machine, taking care, as the oven surfaces will be very hot. Invert the bread pan onto a wire rack and shake several times to dislodge the bread. Allow to cool completely on the rack before slicing or wrapping for storage.

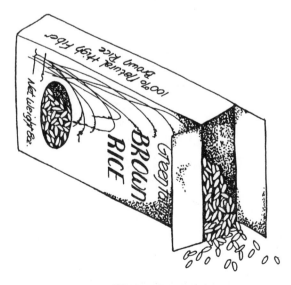

Middle Eastern Chick Pea Bread

INGREDIENT	1-POUND LOAF	1^1/$_2$-POUND LOAF
Whole wheat flour	1^1/$_2$ cups	1^2/$_3$ cups
Bread flour	^{1}/$_2$ cup	^{2}/$_3$ cup
Chick pea flour	^{1}/$_4$ cup	^{1}/$_3$ cup
Gluten flour	^{1}/$_4$ cup	^{1}/$_3$ cup
Dry milk	1 tablespoon	2 tablespoons
Minced fresh cilantro, or dried cilantro	1 tablespoon 1 teaspoon	1^1/$_2$ tablespoons 2 teaspoons
Ground cumin	1^1/$_2$ teaspoons	2 teaspoons
Mashed chick peas	^{1}/$_2$ cup	^{2}/$_3$ cup
Water	1 cup	1^1/$_4$ cups
Sesame oil	2 tablespoons	3 tablespoons
Tahini	1 tablespoon	1^1/$_2$ tablespoons
Honey	1 teaspoon	2 teaspoons
Active dry yeast	1 package	4 teaspoons

This is a lovely golden loaf chock-full of nutrition and taste, and is wonderful served with kabobs, curries, or Middle Eastern salads.

1. Fit the kneading blade firmly on the shaft in the bread pan. Carefully measure the dry ingredients and transfer to the pan. Add the beans, liquid ingredients, and yeast. Place the bread pan inside the machine and close the lid.

2. Program the breadmaker for the whole wheat mode. The unit will begin its operation.

3. At the end of the baking cycle, remove the bread promptly from the machine, taking care, as the oven surfaces will be very hot. Invert the bread pan onto a wire rack and shake several times to dislodge the bread. Allow to cool completely on the rack before slicing or wrapping for storage.

CHAPTER 5

CHEESE, MILK, & EGG BREADS

When you add cheese, milk, or eggs to a bread, you increase its nutritional value and, often, its flavor. While Europeans rarely add these ingredients to their dough, American bakers have been incorporating them into breads for years. All dairy products fortify bread with protein and calcium. Milk, buttermilk, and yogurt also lighten the texture. Bread baked with yogurt has a full, tangy flavor and aroma that are quite appealing. Eggs provide a rich flavor and color, contribute to the bread's rising, and make the texture more cakelike. Cheeses lend their own special flavors.

The delicious recipes in this section range from simple loaves with just a hint of sweetness to some very pronounced cheesy breads that are almost meals in themselves. They are all full-flavored and nutrition-packed. And I hope they inspire you to experiment with your own variations.

$\mathscr{A}$rmenian Bread Rounds

INGREDIENT	1-POUND LOAF	1^1/$_2$-POUND LOAF
Milk	^{1}/$_2$ cup	^{1}/$_2$ cup
Whole wheat flour	1^1/$_4$ cups	1^1/$_2$ cups
Bread flour	1^1/$_4$ cups	1^1/$_2$ cups
Sea salt	1 tablespoon	1^1/$_2$ tablespoons
Water	^{1}/$_2$ cup	^{3}/$_4$ cup
Olive oil	^{1}/$_4$ cup plus 1 tablespoon	^{1}/$_4$ cup plus 2 tablespoons
Honey	2 teaspoons	1 tablespoon
Active dry yeast	1 package	4 teaspoons
Crushed garlic	2 cloves	3 cloves

This recipe comes from Armenia, where the bread is baked on the floor of open ovens. In this savory version, you divide the dough into two pieces, brush the tops with garlic and oil, and bake the rounds on a sheet.

1. In a small saucepan, scald the milk by heating it just to the boiling point, and set aside to cool.

2. Fit the kneading blade firmly on the shaft in the bread pan. Carefully measure the dry ingredients and transfer to the pan. Add the cooled milk, water, 1 tablespoon (or 2 tablespoons) oil, honey, and yeast. Place the bread pan inside the machine and close the lid.

3. Program the breadmaker for the whole wheat dough mode. The unit will begin its operation.

4. At the end of the rising cycle, turn the bread out onto a lightly floured surface. Cover the dough and let it rest for 10 minutes. In a small bowl, combine 1/4 cup olive oil with the crushed garlic. Set aside.

5. Divide the dough into 2 pieces and, with a floured rolling pin, roll each into a 1-inch-thick round. Lightly oil a large baking sheet and arrange the rounds on the sheet. Brush each liberally with some of the garlic oil.

6. Bake the rounds in the lower third of a preheated 375°F oven for 45 minutes, or until golden. Serve warm.

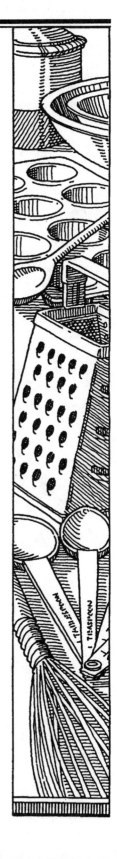

Asiago Bubble Bread

INGREDIENT	1-POUND LOAF	1^1/$_2$-POUND LOAF
Whole wheat flour	1^3/$_4$ cups	2 cups
Bread flour	^{3}/$_4$ cup	1 cup
Grated Asiago or Parmesan cheese	^{1}/$_2$ cup	^{3}/$_4$ cup
Dry milk	^{1}/$_4$ cup	^{1}/$_3$ cup
Sea salt	1 teaspoon	1^1/$_2$ teaspoons
Water	^{2}/$_3$ cup	^{7}/$_8$ cup
Egg(s), beaten	1 large	2 large
Olive oil	^{1}/$_4$ cup plus 1 tablespoon	^{1}/$_4$ cup plus 2 tablespoons
Honey	1 tablespoon	2 tablespoons
Active dry yeast	1 package	4 teaspoons
Crushed garlic	2 cloves	3 cloves
Minced fresh basil, or dried basil	1 tablespoon 1 teaspoon	2 tablespoons 2 teaspoons

I cannot decide if this bread is fun to eat because of its flavor or because of its shape. Children especially like pulling apart the individual bubbles.

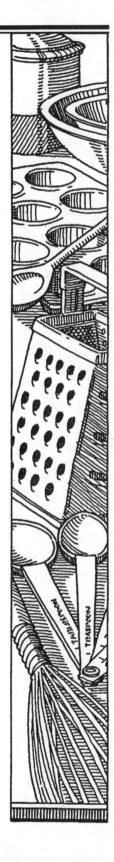

1. Fit the kneading blade firmly on the shaft in the bread pan. Carefully measure the flours, grated cheese, dry milk, and sea salt, and transfer to the pan. Add the water, the egg, 1 tablespoon (or 2 tablespoons) oil, the honey, and the yeast. Place the bread pan inside the machine and close the lid.

2. Program the breadmaker for the whole wheat dough mode. The unit will begin its operation.

3. At the end of the rising cycle, turn the dough out onto a lightly floured surface. Cover the dough and let it rest for 10 minutes. In a shallow bowl, combine 1/4 cup oil with the crushed garlic and basil. Set aside.

4. Lightly oil an 8- or 9-inch round cake pan. Divide the dough into 10 (or 14) pieces and shape each into a ball. Roll each ball in the garlic and oil and place in the pan. Cover and let rise for 30 minutes. Bake the bubble in a preheated 400°F oven for 30 minutes, or until golden brown. Allow to cool for 10 minutes before serving warm.

Beer, Cheese, and Herb Bread

INGREDIENT	1-POUND LOAF	1^1/2-POUND LOAF
Whole wheat flour	2^1/4 cups	2^2/3 cups
Gluten flour	^{1}/4 cup	^{1}/3 cup
Shredded Cheshire or sharp Cheddar cheese	1 cup	1^1/2 cups
Dry milk	1 tablespoon	2 tablespoons
Date sugar	1 tablespoon	1^1/2 tablespoons
Bouquet garni	1 tablespoon	1^1/2 tablespoons
Beer, flat and at room temperature	1 cup	1^1/4 cups
Olive oil	1 tablespoon	2 tablespoons
Active dry yeast	1 package	4 teaspoons

Try to find English Cheshire cheese in a cheese shop or in your market, as it will impart the perfect flavor to this light and crusty bread. If Cheshire is not available, a good sharp Cheddar will be an acceptable substitute.

1. Fit the kneading blade firmly on the shaft in the bread pan. Carefully measure the dry ingredients and transfer to the pan. Add the liquid ingredients and yeast. Place the bread pan inside the machine and close the lid.

2. Program the breadmaker for the whole wheat mode. The unit will begin its operation.

3. At the end of the baking cycle, remove the bread promptly from the machine, taking care, as the oven surfaces will be very hot. Invert the bread pan onto a wire rack and shake several times to dislodge the bread. Allow to cool completely on the rack before slicing or wrapping for storage.

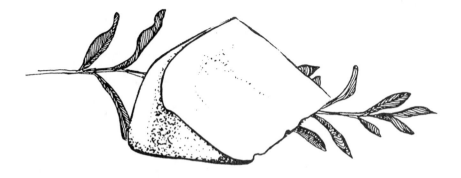

$\mathcal{B}$rioche

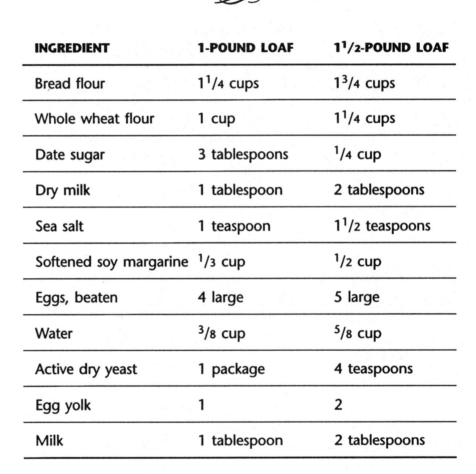

INGREDIENT	1-POUND LOAF	1$^{1}/_{2}$-POUND LOAF
Bread flour	1$^{1}/_{4}$ cups	1$^{3}/_{4}$ cups
Whole wheat flour	1 cup	1$^{1}/_{4}$ cups
Date sugar	3 tablespoons	$^{1}/_{4}$ cup
Dry milk	1 tablespoon	2 tablespoons
Sea salt	1 teaspoon	1$^{1}/_{2}$ teaspoons
Softened soy margarine	$^{1}/_{3}$ cup	$^{1}/_{2}$ cup
Eggs, beaten	4 large	5 large
Water	$^{3}/_{8}$ cup	$^{5}/_{8}$ cup
Active dry yeast	1 package	4 teaspoons
Egg yolk	1	2
Milk	1 tablespoon	2 tablespoons

There are few things more typically French than brioche. This very rich, somewhat sweet dough can be made in one large round loaf or formed into rolls.

1. Fit the kneading blade firmly on the shaft in the bread pan. Carefully measure the dry ingredients and transfer to the pan. Add the margarine, eggs, water, and yeast. Place the bread pan inside the machine and close the lid.

2. Program the breadmaker for the whole wheat dough mode. The unit will begin its operation.

3. At the end of the rising cycle, transfer the dough to an oiled bowl. Brush the top of the dough with oil and chill, tightly covered, for 12 hours.

4. Lightly oil 6 (or 8) muffin cups. Lightly beat the egg yolk and milk together. Turn the dough out onto a well-floured surface and divide into 6 (or 8) pieces. Working quickly, as it soon will become too soft to handle, cut off one-quarter of each piece of dough. Roll each of the larger pieces into a ball and fit into a muffin tin. Brush each with some of the egg yolk mixture. Form each of the smaller pieces of dough into a ball and firmly place each on top of a larger ball. Brush with more egg yolk and set aside in a warm place for 30 minutes.

5. Bake the rolls in a preheated 400°F oven for 20 minutes. Remove from the cups and cool on wire racks. Makes 6 (or 8) rolls.

Challah

INGREDIENT	1-POUND LOAF	1$\frac{1}{2}$-POUND LOAF
Whole wheat flour	1$\frac{3}{4}$ cups	2 cups
Bread flour	$\frac{1}{2}$ cup	$\frac{2}{3}$ cup
Soy flour	$\frac{1}{4}$ cup	$\frac{1}{3}$ cup
Popcorn flour	$\frac{1}{4}$ cup	$\frac{1}{3}$ cup
Sea salt	1 teaspoon	1$\frac{1}{2}$ teaspoons
Water	$\frac{3}{4}$ cup	$\frac{7}{8}$ cup
Eggs, beaten	2 large	3 large
Canola, safflower, or sunflower oil	1$\frac{1}{2}$ tablespoons	3 tablespoons
Honey	1$\frac{1}{2}$ teaspoons	1 tablespoon
Active dry yeast	1 package	4 teaspoons

Here you create and bake the challah in your breadmaker, although you can easily follow the directions for Sweet Challah (page 150), form the dough into a braided loaf, and bake it using traditional methods.

1. Fit the kneading blade firmly on the shaft in the bread pan. Carefully measure the dry ingredients and transfer to the pan. Add the liquid ingredients and yeast. Place the bread pan inside the machine and close the lid.

2. Program the breadmaker for the whole wheat mode. The unit will begin its operation.

3. At the end of the baking cycle, remove the bread promptly from the machine, taking care, as the oven surfaces will be very hot. Invert the bread pan onto a wire rack and shake several times to dislodge the bread. Allow to cool completely on the rack before slicing or wrapping for storage.

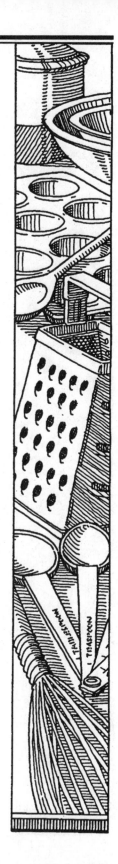

Cheese and Herb Bread

INGREDIENT	1-POUND LOAF	1½-POUND LOAF
Shredded sharp Cheddar cheese	1 cup	1½ cups
Whole wheat flour	1 cup	1¼ cups
Bread flour	1 cup	1¼ cups
Whole rye flour	½ cup	½ cup
Dry milk	1 tablespoon	2 tablespoons
Date sugar	1 tablespoon	2 tablespoons
Crushed garlic	1 clove	2 cloves
Minced fresh oregano, or dried oregano	2 teaspoons / ¾ teaspoon	1 tablespoon / 1 teaspoon
Minced fresh basil, or dried basil	2 teaspoons / ¾ teaspoon	1 tablespoon / 1 teaspoon
Minced fresh rosemary, or dried rosemary	2 teaspoons / ½ teaspoon	1 tablespoon / 1 teaspoon
Sea salt	1 teaspoon	1½ teaspoons
Water	1 cup	1¼ cups

This savory bread has a terrific flavor and a nice crusty exterior.

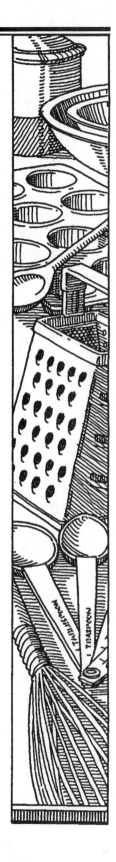

INGREDIENT	1-POUND LOAF	1½-POUND LOAF
Canola, safflower, or sunflower oil	1 tablespoon	2 tablespoons
Active dry yeast	1 package	4 teaspoons

1. Fit the kneading blade firmly on the shaft in the bread pan. Carefully measure the dry ingredients and transfer to the pan. Add the liquid ingredients and the yeast. Place the bread pan inside the machine and close the lid.

2. Program the breadmaker for the whole wheat mode. The unit will begin its operation.

3. At the end of the baking cycle, remove the bread promptly from the machine, taking care, as the oven surfaces will be very hot. Invert the bread pan onto a wire rack and shake several times to dislodge the bread. Allow to cool completely on the rack before slicing or wrapping for storage.

Children's Bread

INGREDIENT	1-POUND LOAF	1^1/$_2$-POUND LOAF
Bread flour	1 cup	1^1/$_4$ cups
Whole wheat flour	1 cup	1^1/$_4$ cups
Gluten flour	^{1}/$_4$ cup	^{1}/$_4$ cup
Graham flour	^{1}/$_4$ cup	^{1}/$_4$ cup
Dry milk	^{1}/$_4$ cup	^{1}/$_3$ cup
Date sugar	2 tablespoons	3 tablespoons
Grated orange zest	1 teaspoon	2 teaspoons
Sea salt	1 teaspoon	1^1/$_2$ teaspoons
Ground nutmeg	^{1}/$_2$ teaspoon	1 teaspoon
Lowfat cottage cheese	^{1}/$_2$ cup	^{2}/$_3$ cup
Eggs, beaten	2 large	3 large
Milk	3 tablespoons	^{1}/$_4$ cup
Maple syrup	2 tablespoons	3 tablespoons
Maple or vanilla extract	^{1}/$_2$ teaspoon	^{3}/$_4$ teaspoon
Active dry yeast	1 package	4 teaspoons

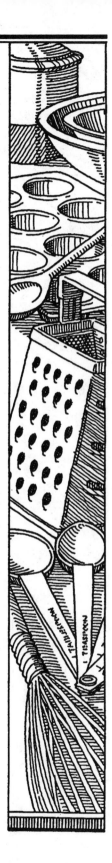

I chose this name because of the bread's high nutritional value and simple, uncomplicated taste. Be sure not to use an automatic timer, as this loaf contains a lot of ingredients that could spoil.

1. Fit the kneading blade firmly on the shaft in the bread pan. Carefully measure the dry ingredients and transfer to the pan. Add the liquid ingredients and the yeast. Place the bread pan inside the machine and close the lid.

2. Program the breadmaker for the whole wheat mode. The unit will begin its operation.

3. At the end of the baking cycle, remove the bread promptly from the machine, taking care, as the oven surfaces will be very hot. Invert the bread pan onto a wire rack and shake several times to dislodge the bread. Allow to cool completely on the rack before slicing or wrapping for storage.

Chili, Cheese, Corn, and Pepper Bread

INGREDIENT	1-POUND LOAF	1¹/2-POUND LOAF
Whole wheat flour	1$\frac{1}{2}$ cups	1$\frac{3}{4}$ cups
Bread flour	1 cup	1$\frac{1}{4}$ cups
Shredded sharp Cheddar cheese	1 cup	1$\frac{1}{2}$ cups
Cooked corn kernels, well drained and blotted dry	$\frac{1}{2}$ cup	$\frac{3}{4}$ cup
Minced red bell pepper	$\frac{1}{3}$ cup	$\frac{1}{2}$ cup
Minced green bell pepper	$\frac{1}{3}$ cup	$\frac{1}{2}$ cup
Dry milk	1 tablespoon	1$\frac{1}{2}$ tablespoons
Chili powder	2 teaspoons	1 tablespoon
Date sugar	2 teaspoons	1 tablespoon
Minced jalapeño chilies	1 teaspoon, or to taste	2 teaspoons, or to taste
Sea salt	1 teaspoon	1$\frac{1}{2}$ teaspoons
Olive oil	1 tablespoon	1$\frac{1}{2}$ tablespoons

Loaded with savory things, this deep orange loaf gets its color from the chili powder.

INGREDIENT	1-POUND LOAF	1¹/₂-POUND LOAF
Water	$^7/_8$ cup	1 cup plus 2 tablespoons
Active dry yeast	1 package	4 teaspoons

1. Fit the kneading blade firmly on the shaft in the bread pan. Carefully measure the flours, cheese, corn, bell peppers, dry milk, chili powder, date sugar, jalapeño chilies, and salt, and transfer to the pan. Add the oil, water, and yeast. Place the bread pan inside the machine and close the lid.

2. Program the breadmaker for the whole wheat mode. The unit will begin its operation.

3. At the end of the baking cycle, remove the bread promptly from the machine, taking care, as the oven surfaces will be very hot. Invert the bread pan onto a wire rack and shake several times to dislodge the bread. Allow to cool completely on the rack before slicing or wrapping for storage.

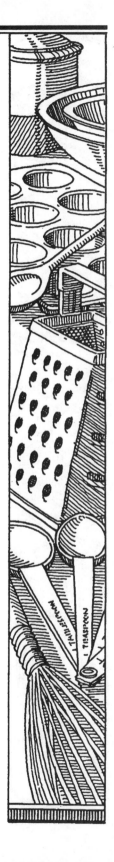

Cottage Dilly Bread

INGREDIENT	1-POUND LOAF	1$\frac{1}{2}$-POUND LOAF
Bread flour	2$\frac{1}{4}$ cups	3 cups
Snipped fresh dill, or dried dillweed	$\frac{1}{4}$ cup 2 tablespoons	6 tablespoons 3 tablespoons
Dry milk	1 tablespoon	2 tablespoons
Sea salt	1 teaspoon	1$\frac{1}{2}$ teaspoons
Water	$\frac{2}{3}$ cup	$\frac{3}{4}$ cup
Lowfat cottage cheese	6 tablespoons	$\frac{1}{2}$ cup
Canola, safflower, or sunflower oil	1 tablespoon	2 tablespoons
Honey	1 teaspoon	2 teaspoons
Active dry yeast	2 teaspoons	1 package

Chili Kidney Bean Bread (page 112) Filled With Red Onion, Sprouts, Avocado, and Cheddar Cheese

Top: Onion Bread Sticks (page 232)
Center Right: Chili, Cheese, Corn,
*   and Pepper Bread (page 134)*
Center Left: Asiago Bubble Bread (page 122)

I like to slice this bread thick and use it for French toast, as it has a mild taste and a pleasing texture. This recipe makes great rolls, too.

1. Fit the kneading blade firmly on the shaft in the bread pan. Carefully measure the dry ingredients and transfer to the pan. Add the liquid ingredients and the yeast. Place the bread pan inside the machine and close the lid.

2. Program the breadmaker for the whole wheat mode. The unit will begin its operation.

3. At the end of the baking cycle, remove the bread promptly from the machine, taking care, as the oven surfaces will be very hot. Invert the bread pan onto a wire rack and shake several times to dislodge the bread. Allow to cool completely on the rack before slicing or wrapping for storage.

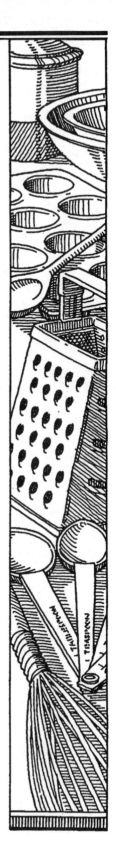

Danish Bread

INGREDIENT	1-POUND LOAF	1^1/$_2$-POUND LOAF
Milk	^{1}/$_2$ cup	^{1}/$_2$ cup
Bread flour	1^1/$_2$ cups	1^3/$_4$ cups
Whole wheat flour	1 cup	1^1/$_4$ cups
Toasted and chopped walnuts	3 tablespoons	^{1}/$_4$ cup
Toasted and chopped almonds	3 tablespoons	^{1}/$_4$ cup
Grated orange zest	1 tablespoon	2 tablespoons
Grated lemon zest	1 tablespoon	2 tablespoons
Dry milk	1 tablespoon	2 tablespoons
Water	^{1}/$_2$ cup	^{3}/$_4$ cup
Canola, safflower, or sunflower oil	1 tablespoon	2 tablespoons
Honey	1 teaspoon	1 teaspoon
Vanilla extract	1 teaspoon	1^1/$_2$ teaspoons
Active dry yeast	1 package	4 teaspoons

Almonds, walnuts, and orange and lemon zest go into this unusual bread, which is just perfect with jam and your morning coffee or tea.

1. In a small saucepan, scald the milk by heating it just to the boiling point, and set aside to cool.

2. Fit the kneading blade firmly on the shaft in the bread pan. Carefully measure the dry ingredients and transfer to the pan. Add the cooled milk, water, oil, honey, extract, and yeast. Place the bread pan inside the machine and close the lid.

3. Program the breadmaker for the whole wheat mode. The unit will begin its operation.

4. At the end of the baking cycle, remove the bread promptly from the machine, taking care, as the oven surfaces will be very hot. Invert the bread pan onto a wire rack and shake several times to dislodge the bread. Allow to cool completely on the rack before slicing or wrapping for storage.

Egg Bread

INGREDIENT	1-POUND LOAF	1^1/$_2$-POUND LOAF
Milk	^{1}/$_4$ cup	^{1}/$_4$ cup
Whole wheat flour	1^1/$_4$ cups	1^1/$_2$ cups
Bread flour	1 cup	1^1/$_4$ cups
Graham flour	^{1}/$_4$ cup	^{1}/$_4$ cup
Dry milk	2 tablespoons	3 tablespoons
Sea salt	1 teaspoon	1^1/$_2$ teaspoons
Water	^{3}/$_8$ cup	^{1}/$_2$ cup
Eggs, beaten	2 large	3 large
Canola, safflower, or sunflower oil	1 tablespoon	2 tablespoons
Honey	1 tablespoon	1 tablespoon
Active dry yeast	2 teaspoons	1 package

You will get a very high, light, and airy bread from this recipe, as well as a lot of nutrition in every bite.

1. In a small saucepan, scald the milk by heating it just to the boiling point, and set aside to cool.

2. Fit the kneading blade firmly on the shaft in the bread pan. Carefully measure the dry ingredients and transfer to the pan. Add the cooled milk, water, eggs, oil, honey, and yeast. Place the bread pan inside the machine and close the lid.

3. Program the breadmaker for the whole wheat mode. The unit will begin its operation.

4. At the end of the baking cycle, remove the bread promptly from the machine, taking care, as the oven surfaces will be very hot. Invert the bread pan onto a wire rack and shake several times to dislodge the bread. Allow to cool completely on the rack before slicing or wrapping for storage.

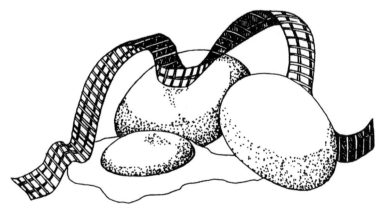

$\mathcal{F}$eta Dill Bread

INGREDIENT	1-POUND LOAF	1^1/$_2$-POUND LOAF
Whole wheat flour	1^1/$_4$ cups	1^1/$_2$ cups
Bread flour	1^1/$_4$ cups	1^1/$_2$ cups
Gluten flour	1 tablespoon	2 tablespoons
Crumbled feta cheese	^{3}/$_4$ cup	1^1/$_2$ cups
Snipped fresh dill, or dried dillweed	^{1}/$_4$ cup 2 tablespoons	^{1}/$_3$ cup 3 tablespoons
Dry milk	1 tablespoon	1 tablespoon
Sea salt	^{1}/$_2$ teaspoon	1 teaspoon
Water	^{1}/$_2$ cup	^{1}/$_2$ cup plus 2 tablespoons
Buttermilk	^{1}/$_2$ cup	^{1}/$_2$ cup plus 2 tablespoons
Canola, safflower, or sunflower oil	1 tablespoon	2 tablespoons
Honey	1 teaspoon	2 teaspoons
Active dry yeast	1 package	4 teaspoons

An imported feta cheese is much better than a domestic cheese in this bread, as it has a more definite flavor that will not be overwhelmed by the other ingredients.

1. Fit the kneading blade firmly on the shaft in the bread pan. Carefully measure the dry ingredients and transfer to the pan. Add the liquid ingredients and the yeast. Place the bread pan inside the machine and close the lid.

2. Program the breadmaker for the whole wheat mode. The unit will begin its operation.

3. At the end of the baking cycle, remove the bread promptly from the machine, taking care, as the oven surfaces will be very hot. Invert the bread pan onto a wire rack and shake several times to dislodge the bread. Allow to cool completely on the rack before slicing or wrapping for storage.

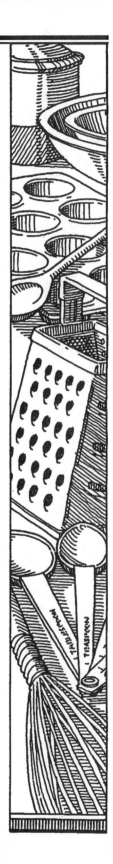

Garlic Asiago Bread

INGREDIENT	1-POUND LOAF	1¹/₂-POUND LOAF
Whole wheat flour	1¹/₂ cups	1³/₄ cups
Bread flour	³/₄ cup	1 cup
Gluten flour	¹/₄ cup	¹/₄ cup
Grated Asiago or Parmesan cheese	¹/₂ cup	³/₄ cup
Dry milk	1 tablespoon	2 tablespoons
Crushed garlic	2 cloves	3 cloves
Minced fresh basil, or dried basil	2 teaspoons ³/₄ teaspoon	1 tablespoon 1 teaspoon
Minced fresh oregano, or dried oregano	1¹/₂ teaspoons ¹/₂ teaspoon	2 teaspoons ³/₄ teaspoon
Minced fresh rosemary, or dried rosemary	1 teaspoon ¹/₄ teaspoon	2 teaspoons ¹/₂ teaspoon
Sea salt	1 teaspoon	1¹/₂ teaspoons
Water	1 cup	1¹/₄ cups
Olive oil	1 tablespoon	2 tablespoons

The only way to describe this bread is "perfect": perfect shape, perfect texture, perfect flavor. An all-around perfectly scrumptious bread.

INGREDIENT	1-POUND LOAF	1¹/₂-POUND LOAF
Honey	1 teaspoon	1 teaspoon
Active dry yeast	1 package	4 teaspoons

1. Fit the kneading blade firmly on the shaft in the bread pan. Carefully measure the dry ingredients and transfer to the pan. Add the liquid ingredients and the yeast. Place the bread pan inside the machine and close the lid.

2. Program the breadmaker for the whole wheat mode. The unit will begin its operation.

3. At the end of the baking cycle, remove the bread promptly from the machine, taking care, as the oven surfaces will be very hot. Invert the bread pan onto a wire rack and shake several times to dislodge the bread. Allow to cool completely on the rack before slicing or wrapping for storage.

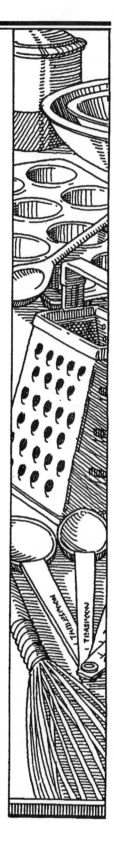

Jalapeño Cheese Bread

INGREDIENT	1-POUND LOAF	1¹/₂-POUND LOAF
Whole wheat flour	1³/₄ cups	2 cups
Bread flour	³/₄ cup	1 cup
Shredded sharp Cheddar cheese	1 cup	1¹/₂ cups
Dry milk	1 tablespoon	1¹/₂ tablespoons
Sea salt	1 teaspoon	1¹/₂ teaspoons
Chili powder	¹/₂ teaspoon	³/₄ teaspoon
Jalapeño chilies, seeded and minced	2, or to taste	3, or to taste
Water	1 cup	1¹/₄ cups
Canola, safflower, or sunflower oil	1 tablespoon	1¹/₂ tablespoons
Honey	1 teaspoon	1¹/₂ teaspoons
Active dry yeast	1 package	4 teaspoons

 *THE BREAD MACHINE GOURMET*

Let your taste buds determine just how hot you like your bread—then adjust the amount of jalapeño chilies to suit your preference.

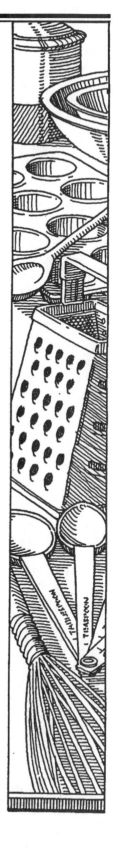

1. Fit the kneading blade firmly on the shaft in the bread pan. Carefully measure the dry ingredients and transfer to the pan. Add the liquid ingredients and the yeast. Place the bread pan inside the machine and close the lid.

2. Program the breadmaker for the whole wheat mode. The unit will begin its operation.

3. At the end of the baking cycle, remove the bread promptly from the machine, taking care, as the oven surfaces will be very hot. Invert the bread pan onto a wire rack and shake several times to dislodge the bread. Allow to cool completely on the rack before slicing or wrapping for storage.

Onion and Cheese Pinwheels

INGREDIENT	1-POUND LOAF	1¹/₂-POUND LOAF
Finely chopped sweet yellow onion	1 cup	1¹/₂ cups
Olive oil	2 tablespoons	3 tablespoons
Whole wheat flour	2¹/₂ cups	3 cups
Dry milk	1 tablespoon	2 tablespoons
Sea salt	1 teaspoon	1¹/₂ teaspoons
Water	1 cup	1¹/₄ cups
Canola, safflower, or sunflower oil	1 tablespoon	2 tablespoons
Honey	1 teaspoon	2 teaspoons
Active dry yeast	1 package	4 teaspoons
Shredded Swiss or Emmenthaler cheese	1¹/₂ cups	2 cups

Almost any one of the simple dough recipes lends itself to these tender rolls, which are filled with onions and cheese. In this recipe, I have used a wheat dough, but I suggest you experiment with other doughs, too.

1. In a medium skillet, sauté the onions in the olive oil until golden brown, about 10 minutes. Remove from the heat and set aside to cool.

2. Fit the kneading blade firmly on the shaft in the bread pan. Carefully measure the flour, dry milk, and salt, and transfer to the pan. Add the water, oil, honey, and yeast. Place the bread pan inside the machine and close the lid.

3. Program the breadmaker for the whole wheat dough mode. The unit will begin its operation.

4. At the end of the rising cycle, turn the dough out onto a lightly floured surface. Cover the dough and let it rest for 10 minutes. With a floured rolling pin, roll the dough into a $1/2$-inch-thick rectangle. Cover the dough with the cooked onions and sprinkle with the shredded cheese.

5. Starting at one of the long sides, roll the dough up tightly, firmly pressing the seam and pinching the ends together. With a sharp knife, cut the roll into 6 (or 9) 2-inch slices. Lightly oil a square or round 8-inch (or 9-inch) baking pan and arrange the rolls, cut sides up. Cover the pan and set aside in a warm place for 20 minutes. Bake in a preheated 350°F oven for 25 minutes, or until golden. Serve hot. Makes 6 (or 9) rolls.

$\mathscr{S}$weet Challah

INGREDIENT	1-POUND LOAF	1$\frac{1}{2}$-POUND LOAF
Bread flour	1$\frac{1}{2}$ cups	1$\frac{3}{4}$ cups
Whole wheat flour	1 cup	1$\frac{1}{4}$ cups
Dry milk	1 tablespoon	2 tablespoons
Sea salt	1 teaspoon	1$\frac{1}{2}$ teaspoons
Water	$\frac{1}{2}$ cup plus 2 tablespoons	$\frac{3}{4}$ cup
Unsweetened apple butter	$\frac{1}{4}$ cup	$\frac{1}{3}$ cup
Honey	2 tablespoons	3 tablespoons
Active dry yeast	2 teaspoons	1 package
Egg(s)	1 large	2 large
Milk	1 teaspoon	2 teaspoons

$\mathscr{T}$HE BREAD MACHINE GOURMET

The apple butter gives this sweet bread a moist, rich taste. If you add $^1/_4$ cup of golden raisins and the same amount of chopped nuts, it's almost a cake.

1. Fit the kneading blade firmly on the shaft in the bread pan. Carefully measure the dry ingredients and transfer to the pan. Add the water, apple butter, honey, and yeast. Place the bread pan inside the machine and close the lid.

2. Program the breadmaker for the whole wheat dough mode. The unit will begin its operation.

3. At the end of the rising cycle, turn the dough out onto a lightly floured surface. Divide the dough into 4 pieces. With floured hands, roll each piece into a 6-inch rope. Lightly oil a large baking sheet. Place the 4 ropes side by side on the baking sheet and lightly pinch them together at one end. Braid the ropes. Lightly pinch the ropes together at the other end.

4. Cover the dough and let rise in a warm place for 30 minutes. In a small bowl, whip together the egg(s) and milk and brush the top of the dough with the mixture. Bake the challah in a preheated 350°F oven for 20 to 25 minutes, or until golden brown.

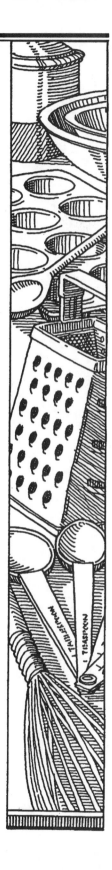

Vienna Bread

INGREDIENT	1-POUND LOAF	1½-POUND LOAF
Milk	½ cup	½ cup
Bread flour	1½ cups	1¾ cups
Whole wheat flour	1 cup	1¼ cups
Date sugar	1 tablespoon	2 tablespoons
Sea salt	1 teaspoon	1½ teaspoons
Water	½ cup	¾ cup
Canola, safflower, or sunflower oil	1 tablespoon	2 tablespoons
Active dry yeast	2 teaspoons	1 package
Yellow cornmeal	1 tablespoon	2 tablespoons
Egg white(s), beaten until frothy	1	2

To produce its characteristic crisp crust and unique flavor, this bread is baked an especially long time.

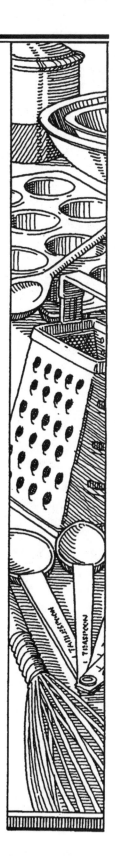

1. In a small saucepan, scald the milk by heating it just to the boiling point, and set aside to cool.

2. Fit the kneading blade firmly on the shaft in the bread pan. Carefully measure the flours, sugar, and salt, and transfer to the pan. Add the cooled milk, water, oil, and yeast. Place the bread pan inside the machine and close the lid.

3. Program the breadmaker for the whole wheat dough mode. The unit will begin its operation.

4. Lightly oil a large baking sheet and sprinkle with cornmeal. At the end of the rising cycle, turn the bread out onto the baking sheet and shape into a round or oval loaf. With a very sharp knife, slash the top in several places. Cover and let the loaf rise for 40 minutes.

5. Lightly brush the top of the loaf with egg white(s) and bake in a preheated 450°F oven for 10 minutes. Reduce the heat to 350°F, brush the top again, and bake for 50 minutes longer. Brush the top of the loaf once more and bake for another 30 minutes. Transfer to a wire rack and allow to cool.

CHAPTER 6

Fruit, Nut, & Chocolate Breads

hile raisin bread will always be an international favorite with children and grown-ups alike, there are many other fruits that you can add to a simple yeast dough. In this chapter, I offer my favorite recipes, all of which produce consistently delicious results. Most of them will be equally successful when substitute ingredients are used, so feel free to try whatever fruit you have on hand. Be sure, however, not to substitute a dried fruit for a fresh one, as the specified amount of water may not be appropriate for the substitute.

Each fruit lends a bread a particular character, texture, and sweetness. Dried fruit, for instance, gives the bread a heartier body, while fresh fruit adds moisture. Ground nuts add texture and infuse the bread with subtle flavor. Chopped nuts make for delightfully crunchy discoveries. I suggest toasting nuts before adding them to enhance the nuts' flavor and, in the case of walnuts, to eliminate some of their bitterness.

The Bread Machine Gourmet

In Chapter 10, beginning on page 271, I suggest a few glazes that may be used to adorn these breads once they have been removed from the breadmaker and cooled. If you glaze a loaf and later wish to toast slices, you can prevent the glaze from melting in the toaster by inserting two or three toothpicks through each slice of bread just under the top crust. The toothpicks will prevent the slice from dropping all the way into the toaster.

Chapter 10 also contains many tantalizing accompaniments to these breads. I think these breads are special enough to be eaten by themselves, yet there are times when spreading the bread with a creamy cheese will make it substantial enough to be a meal or will transport a simple, unassuming bread to intriguing new heights.

Apple Oat Bread

INGREDIENT	1-POUND LOAF	1$\frac{1}{2}$-POUND LOAF
Whole wheat flour	1 cup	1$\frac{1}{4}$ cups
Bread flour	$\frac{3}{4}$ cup	1 cup
Rolled oats	$\frac{3}{4}$ cup	$\frac{3}{4}$ cup
Dry milk	1 tablespoon	1$\frac{1}{2}$ tablespoons
Sea salt	1 teaspoon	1$\frac{1}{2}$ teaspoons
Grated lemon zest	1 teaspoon	1$\frac{1}{2}$ teaspoons
Ground cinnamon	$\frac{1}{4}$ teaspoon	$\frac{1}{2}$ teaspoon
Ground nutmeg	$\frac{1}{4}$ teaspoon	$\frac{1}{2}$ teaspoon
Ground cloves	$\frac{1}{8}$ teaspoon	$\frac{1}{4}$ teaspoon
Unsweetened applesauce	$\frac{1}{4}$ cup	$\frac{1}{4}$ cup
Peeled and grated apple	$\frac{1}{3}$ cup (about 1 small)	$\frac{1}{3}$ cup (about 1 small)
Water	$\frac{1}{4}$ cup plus 2 teaspoons	$\frac{1}{4}$ cup plus 3 tablespoons
Apple juice	$\frac{1}{2}$ cup	$\frac{1}{2}$ cup plus 2 teaspoons

Quite scrumptious by itself, this wonderful bread is absolutely delightful when spread with peanut butter and drizzled with honey.

INGREDIENT	1-POUND LOAF	1^1/$_2$-POUND LOAF
Honey	2 tablespoons	2 tablespoons
Canola, safflower, or sunflower oil	1 tablespoon	1 tablespoon
Active dry yeast	1 package	4 teaspoons

1. Fit the kneading blade firmly on the shaft in the bread pan. Carefully measure the dry ingredients and transfer to the pan. Add the liquid ingredients and yeast. Place the bread pan inside the machine and close the lid.

2. Program the breadmaker for the whole wheat mode. The unit will begin its operation.

3. At the end of the baking cycle, remove the bread promptly from the machine, taking care, as the oven surfaces will be very hot. Invert the bread pan onto a wire rack and shake several times to dislodge the bread. Allow to cool completely on the rack before slicing or wrapping for storage.

$\mathcal{A}$pricot Spice Bread

INGREDIENT	1-POUND LOAF	1^1/$_2$-POUND LOAF
Dried apricots	^{1}/$_2$ cup	^{2}/$_3$ cup
Water	^{1}/$_2$ cup	^{2}/$_3$ cup
Bread flour	2^1/$_4$ cups	3 cups
Dry milk	1 tablespoon	1^1/$_2$ tablespoons
Sea salt	1 teaspoon	1^1/$_2$ teaspoons
Ground cinnamon	^{1}/$_4$ teaspoon	^{1}/$_2$ teaspoon
Ground anise seed	^{1}/$_2$ teaspoon	^{3}/$_4$ teaspoon
Ground allspice	^{1}/$_2$ teaspoon	^{3}/$_4$ teaspoon
Apricot nectar	^{3}/$_8$–^{1}/$_2$ cup	^{1}/$_2$–^{3}/$_4$ cup
Canola, safflower, or sunflower oil	1 tablespoon	2 tablespoons
Honey	1 tablespoon	2 tablespoons
Active dry yeast	2 teaspoons	1 package

The apricots and apricot nectar, a delicate combination, produce a wonderful bread with appealing flavors and a warm, peachy color.

1. Place the apricots and water in a small saucepan and bring to a boil. Remove from the heat and allow to steep for 5 minutes. Drain the apricots, reserving the liquid, and spread them out on a double thickness of paper towels. Allow the apricots and the liquid to cool to room temperature.

2. Fit the kneading blade firmly on the shaft in the bread pan. Carefully measure the flour, dry milk, salt, and spices, and transfer to the pan. Measure the reserved cooking liquid and add enough apricot nectar to measure $5/8$ cup (or $7/8$ cup). Add this mixture to the bread pan along with the oil, honey, and yeast. Place the bread pan inside the machine and close the lid.

3. Program the breadmaker for the whole wheat mode. The unit will begin its operation.

4. At the end of the mixing cycle and just before the kneading cycle begins, finely chop the cooled apricots and add them to the dough.

5. At the end of the baking cycle, remove the bread promptly from the machine, taking care, as the oven surfaces will be very hot. Invert the bread pan onto a wire rack and shake several times to dislodge the bread. Allow to cool completely on the rack before slicing or wrapping for storage.

Banana Date Bread

INGREDIENT	1-POUND LOAF	1¹/₂-POUND LOAF
Whole wheat flour	1¹/₂ cups	1²/₃ cups
Bread flour	1 cup	1¹/₃ cups
Date sugar	2 tablespoons	3 tablespoons
Dry milk	1¹/₂ tablespoons	2 tablespoons
Ground nutmeg	¹/₂ teaspoon	1 teaspoon
Salt	1 teaspoon	1¹/₂ teaspoons
Ground allspice	¹/₄ teaspoon	¹/₂ teaspoon
Ground ginger	¹/₄ teaspoon	¹/₂ teaspoon
Water	⁷/₈ cup	1¹/₄ cups
Canola, safflower, or sunflower oil	2 tablespoons	3 tablespoons
Vanilla extract	1 teaspoon	1¹/₂ teaspoons
Ripe banana, sliced	1 medium	1 large
Active dry yeast	1 package	4 teaspoons
Minced dates	2 tablespoons	3 tablespoons

THE BREAD MACHINE GOURMET

This rich, moist breakfast bread has never survived long enough to cool and be wrapped for storage.

1. Fit the kneading blade firmly on the shaft in the bread pan. Carefully measure the flours, sugar, dry milk, and spices, and transfer to the pan. Add the liquid ingredients, banana, and yeast. Place the bread pan inside the machine and close the lid.

2. Program the breadmaker for the whole wheat mode. The unit will begin its operation.

3. At the end of the mixing cycle and just before the kneading cycle begins, add the dates to the dough.

4. At the end of the baking cycle, remove the bread promptly from the machine, taking care, as the oven surfaces will be very hot. Invert the bread pan onto a wire rack and shake several times to dislodge the bread. Allow to cool completely on the rack before slicing or wrapping for storage.

$\mathcal{B}$anana Maple Bread

INGREDIENT	1-POUND LOAF	1^1/2-POUND LOAF
Whole wheat flour	2^1/4 cups	2^2/3 cups
Graham flour	^{1}/4 cup	^{1}/3 cup
Dry milk	1 tablespoon	2 tablespoons
Grated orange zest	1 tablespoon	1^1/2 tablespoons
Sea salt	1 teaspoon	1^1/2 teaspoons
Ripe banana, sliced	1 large	1^1/2 large
Egg(s), beaten	1 large	2 large
Water	^{1}/4 cup	^{1}/4 cup plus 3 tablespoons
Maple syrup	^{1}/4 cup	^{1}/3 cup
Canola, safflower, or sunflower oil	^{1}/4 cup	^{1}/3 cup
Maple extract	^{1}/2 teaspoon	1 teaspoon
Active dry yeast	1 package	4 teaspoons

This sweet, flavorful bread derives much of its appeal from the maple extract, which gives it a pronounced maple flavor.

1. Fit the kneading blade firmly on the shaft in the bread pan. Carefully measure the flours, dry milk, orange zest, and salt, and transfer to the pan. Add the banana, liquid ingredients, and yeast. Place the bread pan inside the machine and close the lid.

2. Program the breadmaker for the whole wheat mode. The unit will begin its operation.

3. At the end of the baking cycle, remove the bread promptly from the machine, taking care, as the oven surfaces will be very hot. Invert the bread pan onto a wire rack and shake several times to dislodge the bread. Allow to cool completely on the rack before slicing or wrapping for storage.

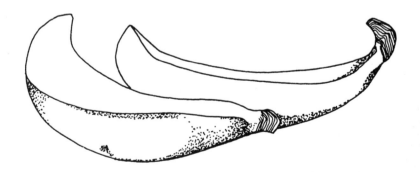

Chocolate Chip and Nut Bread

INGREDIENT	1-POUND LOAF	1½-POUND LOAF
Whole wheat flour	1¼ cups	1½ cups
Bread flour	1¼ cups	1½ cups
Dry milk	1 tablespoon	2 tablespoons
Sea salt	1 teaspoon	1½ teaspoons
Toasted and chopped almonds	¼ cup	⅓ cup
Toasted and ground almonds	¼ cup	⅓ cup
Semisweet chocolate chips	½ cup	⅔ cup
Water	⅞ cup	1 cup plus 3 tablespoons
Honey	2 tablespoons	3 tablespoons
Canola, safflower, or sunflower oil	1 tablespoon	2 tablespoons
Almond extract	½ teaspoon	1 teaspoon
Active dry yeast	1 package	4 teaspoons

*If your weakness is chocolate, you will adore this
beautiful bread with its luscious taste. It is just perfect
on cold winter mornings with a cup of hot chocolate
topped with whipped cream.*

1. Fit the kneading blade firmly
on the shaft in the bread pan. Carefully measure the flours, dry
milk, salt, and nuts, and transfer to the pan. Add the chocolate
chips, liquid ingredients, and yeast. Place the bread pan inside
the machine and close the lid.

2. Program the breadmaker for
the whole wheat mode. The unit will begin its operation.

3. At the end of the baking cycle,
remove the bread promptly from the machine, taking care, as the
oven surfaces will be very hot. Invert the bread pan onto a wire
rack and shake several times to dislodge the bread. Allow to cool
completely on the rack before slicing or wrapping for storage.

Citrus Bread

INGREDIENT	1-POUND LOAF	1^{1}/2-POUND LOAF
Navel orange	1 large	1 large
Whole wheat flour	2^{1}/2 cups	3 cups
Popcorn flour	^{1}/2 cup	^{1}/2 cup
Grated orange zest	1^{1}/2 tablespoons	2 tablespoons
Grated lemon zest	1^{1}/2 tablespoons	2 tablespoons
Sea salt	1 teaspoon	1^{1}/2 teaspoons
Water	^{1}/2 cup	^{3}/4 cup
Canola, safflower, or sunflower oil	3 tablespoons	^{1}/4 cup
Honey	2 tablespoons	3 tablespoons
Active dry yeast	1 package	4 teaspoons

Adding popcorn flour to this bread lightens the whole wheat. The result is a sweet, mellow bread with a distinctive texture.

1. Peel the orange and remove all the white pith and seeds from the flesh. In a blender or food processor, purée the pulp and juice until almost smooth. Measure $1/2$ cup of the pulp and juice and set aside. Discard the remaining pulp.

2. Fit the kneading blade firmly on the shaft in the bread pan. Carefully measure the dry ingredients and transfer to the pan. Add the pulp and juice, water, oil, honey, and yeast. Place the bread pan inside the machine and close the lid.

3. Program the breadmaker for the whole wheat mode. The unit will begin its operation.

4. At the end of the baking cycle, remove the bread promptly from the machine, taking care, as the oven surfaces will be very hot. Invert the bread pan onto a wire rack and shake several times to dislodge the bread. Allow to cool completely on the rack before slicing or wrapping for storage.

Ginger Nut Banana Rolls

INGREDIENT	1-POUND LOAF	1¹/₂-POUND LOAF
Whole wheat flour	1¹/₄ cups	1¹/₂ cups
Bread flour	1¹/₄ cups	1¹/₂ cups
Dry milk	1 tablespoon	2 tablespoons
Ground ginger	2 teaspoons	1 tablespoon
Sea salt	1 teaspoon	1¹/₂ teaspoons
Toasted and chopped walnuts	¹/₄ cup	¹/₃ cup
Ripe banana, sliced	1 medium	1 large
Water	¹/₂ cup plus 1 tablespoon	³/₄ cup
Honey	3 tablespoons	¹/₄ cup
Canola, safflower, or sunflower oil	2 tablespoons	3 tablespoons
Active dry yeast	1 package	4 teaspoons
Egg, beaten	1 large	1 large

 *THE BREAD MACHINE GOURMET*

Top Right: Onion and Cheese Pinwheels (page 148)
Top Left: Ginger Nut Banana Rolls (page 168)
Bottom: Brioche (page 126)

Top: Irish Soda Bread (page 172)
Center: Sweet Challah (page 150)
Bottom: Easter Buns (page 248)

No one flavor dominates in these delectable rolls, which are perfect for Sunday brunches.

1. Fit the kneading blade firmly on the shaft in the bread pan. Carefully measure the flours, dry milk, ginger, salt, walnuts, and banana, and transfer to the pan. Add the water, honey, oil, and yeast. Place the bread pan inside the machine and close the lid.

2. Program the breadmaker for the whole wheat dough mode. The unit will begin its operation.

3. At the end of the rising cycle, turn the dough out onto a floured surface. Cover the dough and let it rest for 10 minutes. Lightly oil a small baking sheet. Divide the dough into 8 (or 11) pieces and, with floured hands, roll each piece into a ball. Place the balls on the prepared baking sheet and cover with a towel. Let the rolls rise in a warm place for 30 minutes.

4. Lightly brush the tops of the rolls with the beaten egg and bake them in a preheated 400°F oven for 15 to 20 minutes, or until golden. Serve warm. Makes 8 (or 11) rolls.

Hazelnut Currant Bread

INGREDIENT	1-POUND LOAF	1$\frac{1}{2}$-POUND LOAF
Whole wheat flour	1$\frac{1}{4}$ cups	1$\frac{2}{3}$ cups
Bread flour	1 cup	1 cup
Whole rye flour	$\frac{1}{4}$ cup	$\frac{1}{3}$ cup
Dry milk	1 tablespoon	2 tablespoons
Sea salt	1 teaspoon	1$\frac{1}{2}$ teaspoons
Water	1 cup	1$\frac{1}{4}$ cups
Soy margarine	2 tablespoons	3 tablespoons
Honey	1 teaspoon	2 teaspoons
Active dry yeast	1 package	4 teaspoons
Toasted and finely chopped hazelnuts	$\frac{1}{3}$ cup	$\frac{1}{2}$ cup
Dried currants	$\frac{1}{4}$ cup	$\frac{1}{3}$ cup

Although well known for its breads, France does not usually bring to mind whole wheat breads. The French make some wonderful whole grain loaves, however, and this recipe is my variation of one of their finest.

1. Fit the kneading blade firmly on the shaft in the bread pan. Carefully measure the flours, dry milk, and salt, and transfer to the pan. Add the water, margarine, honey, and yeast. Place the bread pan inside the machine and close the lid.

2. Program the breadmaker for the whole wheat mode. The unit will begin its operation.

3. At the end of the mixing cycle and just before the kneading cycle begins, add the hazelnuts and currants to the dough.

4. At the end of the baking cycle, remove the bread promptly from the machine, taking care, as the oven surfaces will be very hot. Invert the bread pan onto a wire rack and shake several times to dislodge the bread. Allow to cool completely on the rack before slicing or wrapping for storage.

$\mathcal{I}$rish Soda Bread

INGREDIENT	1-POUND LOAF	1^1/$_2$-POUND LOAF
Golden raisins	^{1}/$_2$ cup	^{2}/$_3$ cup
Water	^{3}/$_4$ cup	1 cup plus 2 tablespoons
Whole wheat flour	1^1/$_2$ cups	1^3/$_4$ cups
Bread flour	1 cup	1^1/$_4$ cups
Date sugar	2 tablespoons	3 tablespoons
Grated lemon zest	1 tablespoon	2 tablespoons
Baking soda	1 teaspoon	1^1/$_2$ teaspoons
Sea salt	1 teaspoon	1^1/$_2$ teaspoons
Egg(s), beaten	1 large	2 large
Canola, safflower, or sunflower oil	2 tablespoons	3 tablespoons
Active dry yeast	1 package	4 teaspoons

Irish soda bread is best eaten the day you make it, which has never been a problem around our house. It works equally well whether made in the breadmaker or prepared as a dough and baked in the oven.

1. Place the raisins and water in a small saucepan and bring to a boil. Turn off the heat and allow to cool. Drain the raisins and set aside, reserving the liquid.

2. Fit the kneading blade firmly on the shaft in the bread pan. Carefully measure the flours, sugar, lemon zest, baking soda, and salt, and transfer to the pan. Add the reserved raisin liquid, egg(s), oil, and yeast. Place the bread pan inside the machine and close the lid.

3. Program the breadmaker for the whole wheat mode. The unit will begin its operation.

4. At the end of the mixing cycle and just before the kneading cycle begins, add the drained raisins to the dough.

5. At the end of the baking cycle, remove the bread promptly from the machine, taking care, as the oven surfaces will be very hot. Invert the bread pan onto a wire rack and shake several times to dislodge the bread. Allow to cool completely on the rack before slicing or wrapping for storage.

Light Nut Bread

INGREDIENT	1-POUND LOAF	1 1/2-POUND LOAF
Bread flour	2 1/4 cups	2 2/3 cups
Oat bran	1/4 cup	1/3 cup
Toasted and finely chopped almonds	2 tablespoons	3 tablespoons
Toasted and ground almonds	2 tablespoons	3 tablespoons
Toasted and finely chopped pecans	2 tablespoons	3 tablespoons
Toasted and ground pecans	2 tablespoons	3 tablespoons
Toasted and finely chopped walnuts	2 tablespoons	3 tablespoons
Toasted and ground walnuts	2 tablespoons	3 tablespoons
Dry milk	1 tablespoon	2 tablespoons
Sea salt	1 teaspoon	1 1/2 teaspoons
Water	7/8 cup	1 1/4 cups
Honey	2 tablespoons	3 tablespoons

Try this high-rising, light, and luscious bread with one of the wonderful spreads found in Chapter 10.

INGREDIENT	1-POUND LOAF	1$^{1}/_{2}$-POUND LOAF
Canola, safflower, or sunflower oil	1 tablespoon	2 tablespoons
Almond extract	1 teaspoon	1$^{1}/_{2}$ teaspoons
Active dry yeast	1 package	4 teaspoons

1. Fit the kneading blade firmly on the shaft in the bread pan. Carefully measure the dry ingredients and transfer to the pan. Add the liquid ingredients and yeast. Place the bread pan inside the machine and close the lid.

2. Program the breadmaker for the whole wheat mode. The unit will begin its operation.

3. At the end of the baking cycle, remove the bread promptly from the machine, taking care, as the oven surfaces will be very hot. Invert the bread pan onto a wire rack and shake several times to dislodge the bread. Allow to cool completely on the rack before slicing or wrapping for storage.

Mandarin Orange Bread

INGREDIENT	1-POUND LOAF	1¹/₂-POUND LOAF
Mandarin oranges in light syrup	1 can (11 ounces)	1¹/₂ cans
Water	¹/₄ –¹/₃ cup	¹/₃–¹/₂ cup
Whole wheat flour	1 cup	1¹/₃ cups
Bread flour	1 cup	1¹/₃ cups
Oat-blend flour	¹/₂ cup	³/₄ cup
Popcorn flour	¹/₄ cup	¹/₃ cup
Dry milk	1 tablespoon	2 tablespoons
Grated orange zest	1 tablespoon	2 tablespoons
Date sugar	1 tablespoon	2 tablespoons
Sea salt	1 teaspoon	1¹/₂ teaspoons
Canola, safflower, or sunflower oil	2 tablespoons	3 tablespoons
Honey	1 tablespoon	2 tablespoons
Active dry yeast	1 package	4 teaspoons
Minced dates	¹/₄ cup	¹/₃ cup

Be sure to add the oranges and dates just before the kneading cycle begins so that the consistency of the dough will be maintained.

1. Drain the oranges well, reserving the liquid. Arrange them on a double thickness of paper towels and lightly pat dry. Set aside. Measure the reserved liquid, adding water until you have $7/8$ cup (or 1 cup plus 2 tablespoons).

2. Fit the kneading blade firmly on the shaft in the bread pan. Carefully measure the flours, dry milk, orange zest, sugar, and salt, and transfer to the pan. Add the combined water and orange liquid, oil, honey, and yeast. Place the bread pan inside the machine and close the lid.

3. Program the breadmaker for the whole wheat mode. The unit will begin its operation.

4. At the end of the mixing cycle and just before the kneading cycle begins, add the drained oranges and the dates to the dough.

5. At the end of the baking cycle, remove the bread promptly from the machine, taking care, as the oven surfaces will be very hot. Invert the bread pan onto a wire rack and shake several times to dislodge the bread. Allow to cool completely on the rack before slicing or wrapping for storage.

$\mathcal{M}$olasses, Currant, and Date Bread

INGREDIENT	1-POUND LOAF	1^1/$_2$-POUND LOAF
Whole wheat flour	1^1/$_4$ cups	1^1/$_2$ cups
Bread flour	1 cup	1^1/$_4$ cups
Oat-blend flour	2 tablespoons	^{1}/$_4$ cup
Gluten flour	2 tablespoons	2 tablespoons
Cocoa or carob powder	3 tablespoons	^{1}/$_4$ cup
Dry milk	1 tablespoon	2 tablespoons
Sea salt	1 teaspoon	1^1/$_2$ teaspoons
Water	^{2}/$_3$ cup	^{3}/$_4$ cup
Amaretto liqueur*	^{1}/$_4$ cup	^{1}/$_4$ cup
Molasses	3 tablespoons	^{1}/$_4$ cup
Honey	1 tablespoon	2 tablespoons
Canola, safflower, or sunflower oil	1 tablespoon	2 tablespoons
Active dry yeast	1 package	4 teaspoons
Dried currants	3 tablespoons	^{1}/$_4$ cup
Chopped dates	3 tablespoons	^{1}/$_4$ cup

*Water can be substituted for the amaretto liqueur, if you wish.

Molasses and cocoa or carob powder add a deep, dark sweetness to this rich, wholesome bread.

1. Fit the kneading blade firmly on the shaft in the bread pan. Carefully measure the flours, cocoa, dry milk, and sea salt, and transfer to the pan. Add the water, amaretto, molasses, honey, oil, and yeast. Place the bread pan inside the machine and close the lid.

2. Program the breadmaker for the whole wheat mode. The unit will begin its operation.

3. At the end of the mixing cycle and just before the kneading cycle begins, add the currants and dates to the dough.

4. At the end of the baking cycle, remove the bread promptly from the machine, taking care, as the oven surfaces will be very hot. Invert the bread pan onto a wire rack and shake several times to dislodge the bread. Allow to cool completely on the rack before slicing or wrapping for storage.

Oatmeal and Fruit Bread

INGREDIENT	1-POUND LOAF	1¹/₂-POUND LOAF
Chopped assorted dried fruit*	¹/₂ cup	²/₃ cup
Water	1 cup	1¹/₄ cups
Whole wheat flour	1 cup	1¹/₄ cups
Bread flour	1 cup	1¹/₄ cups
Rolled oats	¹/₂ cup	¹/₂ cup
Date sugar	2 tablespoons	3 tablespoons
Dry milk	1 tablespoon	2 tablespoons
Grated orange zest	1 tablespoon	2 tablespoons
Sea salt	1 teaspoon	1¹/₂ teaspoons
Ground nutmeg	¹/₂ teaspoon	1 teaspoon
Honey	2 tablespoons	3 tablespoons
Canola, safflower, or sunflower oil	1 tablespoon	2 tablespoons
Active dry yeast	1 package	4 teaspoons

*Almost any combination of dried fruits can be used in this recipe. I have had great success with raisins, currants, apples, apricots, and, one of my favorites, pears. Crushed dried bananas and coconut flakes also add unique flavors.

This great loaf is filled with flavorful dried fruits, and you can use any combination of fruits you have available. This bread is especially good topped with orange marmalade.

1. In a small saucepan, bring the dried fruit and water to a boil. Remove from the heat and allow to steep for 5 minutes. Drain the fruit and set aside, reserving the liquid.

2. Fit the kneading blade firmly on the shaft in the bread pan. Carefully measure the flours, oats, sugar, dry milk, orange zest, salt, and nutmeg, and transfer to the pan. Add the reserved liquid, honey, oil, and yeast. Place the bread pan inside the machine and close the lid.

3. Program the breadmaker for the whole wheat mode. The unit will begin its operation.

4. At the end of the mixing cycle and just before the kneading cycle begins, add the reserved fruit to the dough.

5. At the end of the baking cycle, remove the bread promptly from the machine, taking care, as the oven surfaces will be very hot. Invert the bread pan onto a wire rack and shake several times to dislodge the bread. Allow to cool completely on the rack before slicing or wrapping for storage.

Oatmeal, Raisin, and Honey Bread

INGREDIENT	1-POUND LOAF	1¹/₂-POUND LOAF
Golden raisins	¹/₃ cup	¹/₂ cup
Grated orange zest	1 tablespoon	2 tablespoons
Water	⁷/₈ cup	1 cup plus 1 tablespoon
Whole wheat flour	1³/₄ cups	1³/₄ cups
Oat-blend flour	¹/₂ cup	³/₄ cup
Rolled oats	¹/₄ cup	¹/₂ cup
Dry milk	2 tablespoons	3 tablespoons
Sea salt	1 teaspoon	1¹/₂ teaspoons
Honey	3 tablespoons	¹/₄ cup
Canola, safflower, or sunflower oil	1 tablespoon	2 tablespoons
Active dry yeast	1 package	4 teaspoons

In my kitchen, this bread never has a chance to cool, as it disappears as soon as it comes out of the breadmaker.

1. Place the raisins, orange zest, and water in a small saucepan and bring to a boil. Remove from the heat and set aside to cool. Drain the raisins and zest, reserving the liquid.

2. Fit the kneading blade firmly on the shaft in the bread pan. Carefully measure the flours, oats, dry milk, and sea salt, and transfer to the pan. Add the reserved liquid, honey, oil, and yeast. Place the bread pan inside the machine and close the lid.

3. Program the breadmaker for the whole wheat mode. The unit will begin its operation.

4. At the end of the mixing cycle and just before the kneading cycle begins, add the drained raisins and orange zest to the dough.

5. At the end of the baking cycle, remove the bread promptly from the machine, taking care, as the oven surfaces will be very hot. Invert the bread pan onto a wire rack and shake several times to dislodge the bread. Allow to cool completely on the rack before slicing or wrapping for storage.

Orange Raisin Bread

INGREDIENT	1-POUND LOAF	1^1/$_2$-POUND LOAF
Golden raisins	^{1}/$_2$ cup	^{2}/$_3$ cup
Water	^{1}/$_2$ cup	^{3}/$_4$ cup
Whole wheat flour	1^1/$_2$ cups	1^3/$_4$ cups
Bread flour	^{3}/$_4$ cup	1 cup
Gluten flour	^{1}/$_4$ cup	^{1}/$_4$ cup
Date sugar	2 tablespoons	3 tablespoons
Grated orange zest	1^1/$_2$ tablespoons	2 tablespoons
Dry milk	1 tablespoon	2 tablespoons
Sea salt	1 teaspoon	1^1/$_2$ teaspoons
Ground nutmeg	^{1}/$_2$ teaspoon	^{3}/$_4$ teaspoon
Fresh orange juice	^{1}/$_2$ cup	^{1}/$_2$ cup
Canola, safflower, or sunflower oil	2 tablespoons	3 tablespoons
Vanilla extract	^{1}/$_2$ teaspoon	1 teaspoon
Active dry yeast	1 package	4 teaspoons

THE BREAD MACHINE GOURMET

Simple, uncomplicated, and uncommonly good, this loaf with its hint of orange makes excellent toast.

1. Place the raisins and water in a small saucepan and bring to a boil. Remove from the heat and allow to steep for 5 minutes. Drain the raisins and set aside to cool, reserving the liquid.

2. Fit the kneading blade firmly on the shaft in the bread pan. Carefully measure the flours, sugar, orange zest, dry milk, salt, and nutmeg, and transfer to the pan. Add the reserved liquid, orange juice, oil, vanilla, and yeast. Place the bread pan inside the machine and close the lid.

3. Program the breadmaker for the whole wheat mode. The unit will begin its operation.

4. At the end of the mixing cycle and just before the kneading cycle begins, add the drained raisins to the dough.

5. At the end of the baking cycle, remove the bread promptly from the machine, taking care, as the oven surfaces will be very hot. Invert the bread pan onto a wire rack and shake several times to dislodge the bread. Allow to cool completely on the rack before slicing or wrapping for storage.

*P*an Nero

INGREDIENT	1-POUND LOAF	1¹/₂-POUND LOAF
Unsweetened chocolate	2 squares	3 squares
Soy margarine	1 tablespoon	2 tablespoons
Bread flour	2 cups	2¹/₂ cups
Graham flour	¹/₄ cup	¹/₄ cup
Toasted and ground almonds	¹/₄ cup	¹/₃ cup
Dry milk	1 tablespoon	2 tablespoons
Sea salt	1 teaspoon	1¹/₂ teaspoons
Water	⁵/₈ cup	⁷/₈ cup
Honey	¹/₄ cup	¹/₄ cup plus 1 tablespoon
Egg(s), beaten	1 large	2 large
Active dry yeast	2 teaspoons	1 package

This sweet chocolate loaf is the consummate coffee bread. Serve it cold, perhaps with one of the whips, dips, spreads, or glazes from Chapter 10, and wait for the raves.

1. In a small saucepan, melt the chocolate and margarine together over low heat, and set aside to cool.

2. Fit the kneading blade firmly on the shaft in the bread pan. Carefully measure the dry ingredients and transfer to the pan. Add the cooled chocolate mixture, water, honey, egg(s), and yeast. Place the bread pan inside the machine and close the lid.

3. Program the breadmaker for the white bread mode. The unit will begin its operation.

4. At the end of the baking cycle, remove the bread promptly from the machine, taking care, as the oven surfaces will be very hot. Invert the bread pan onto a wire rack and shake several times to dislodge the bread. Allow to cool completely on the rack before slicing or wrapping for storage.

Peach Orange Bread

INGREDIENT	1-POUND LOAF	1^1/$_2$-POUND LOAF
Whole wheat flour	1^1/$_2$ cups	1^3/$_4$ cups
Bread flour	^{3}/$_4$ cup	1 cup
Gluten flour	^{1}/$_4$ cup	^{1}/$_4$ cup
Date sugar	3 tablespoons	^{1}/$_4$ cup
Dry milk	1 tablespoon	2 tablespoons
Grated orange zest	2 teaspoons	1 tablespoon
Sea salt	1 teaspoon	1^1/$_2$ teaspoons
Pumpkin pie spice	1 teaspoon	1^1/$_2$ teaspoons
Peeled and chopped peach	^{3}/$_4$ cup (about 1 medium)	1 cup (about 1 large)
Water	^{1}/$_2$ cup	^{3}/$_4$ cup
Fresh orange juice	^{1}/$_4$ cup plus 2 tablespoons	^{1}/$_2$ cup
Canola, safflower, or sunflower oil	1 tablespoon	2 tablespoons
Active dry yeast	1 package	4 teaspoons

Try spreading thick slices of this bread with peanut butter or cream cheese and all-fruit peach preserves for an outstanding and scrumptious sandwich.

1. Fit the kneading blade firmly on the shaft in the bread pan. Carefully measure the dry ingredients and transfer to the pan. Add the peach, liquid ingredients, and yeast. Place the bread pan inside the machine and close the lid.

2. Program the breadmaker for the whole wheat mode. The unit will begin its operation.

3. At the end of the baking cycle, remove the bread promptly from the machine, taking care, as the oven surfaces will be very hot. Invert the bread pan onto a wire rack and shake several times to dislodge the bread. Allow to cool completely on the rack before slicing or wrapping for storage.

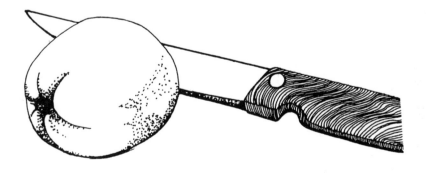

Peanut Butter Bread

INGREDIENT	1-POUND LOAF	1 1/2-POUND LOAF
Bread flour	1 1/2 cups	1 3/4 cups
Whole wheat flour	1 cup	1 1/4 cups
Dry milk	1 tablespoon	2 tablespoons
Sea salt	1 teaspoon	1 1/2 teaspoons
Ground nutmeg	1/2 teaspoon	1 teaspoon
Water	1 cup	1 1/4 cups
Chunky peanut butter	3 tablespoons	5 tablespoons
Honey	2 tablespoons	3 tablespoons
Vanilla extract	1 teaspoon	1 1/2 teaspoons
Active dry yeast	1 package	4 teaspoons

For the ultimate in peanut butter madness, spread this light bread with Peanut Butter Cheese (page 293).

1. Fit the kneading blade firmly on the shaft in the bread pan. Carefully measure the dry ingredients and transfer to the pan. Add the water, peanut butter, honey, vanilla, and yeast. Place the bread pan inside the machine and close the lid.

2. Program the breadmaker for the whole wheat mode. The unit will begin its operation.

3. At the end of the baking cycle, remove the bread promptly from the machine, taking care, as the oven surfaces will be very hot. Invert the bread pan onto a wire rack and shake several times to dislodge the bread. Allow to cool completely on the rack before slicing or wrapping for storage.

Raisin and Soy Bread

INGREDIENT	1-POUND LOAF	1½-POUND LOAF
Golden raisins	½ cup	⅔ cup
Water	¾–⅞ cup	1–1¼ cups
Whole wheat flour	2 cups	2¼ cups
Semolina	¼ cup	¼ cup plus 2 tablespoons
Soy flour	2 tablespoons	3 tablespoons
Gluten flour	1 tablespoon	2 tablespoons
Date sugar	2 tablespoons	3 tablespoons
Dry milk	1 tablespoon	2 tablespoons
Soy flakes	1 tablespoon	1 tablespoon
Sea salt	1 teaspoon	1½ teaspoons
Amaretto liqueur*	2 tablespoons	3 tablespoons
Canola, safflower, or sunflower oil	2 tablespoons	3 tablespoons
Active dry yeast	1 package	4 teaspoons

*Water can be substituted for the amaretto, if you wish.

This honey-colored loaf is light and nutritious, with just a trace of sweetness.

1. In a small saucepan, bring the raisins and $1/2$ cup of the water to a boil. Remove from the heat and allow to steep for 5 minutes. Strain the raisins and allow to cool, reserving the liquid.

2. Fit the kneading blade firmly on the shaft in the bread pan. Carefully measure the flours, sugar, dry milk, soy flakes, and salt, and transfer to the pan. To the reserved liquid, add enough water to measure $3/4$ cup plus 1 tablespoon (or $15/16$ cup). Add the liquid, amaretto, oil, and yeast to the bread pan. Place the bread pan inside the machine and close the lid.

3. Program the breadmaker for the whole wheat mode. The unit will begin its operation.

4. At the end of the mixing cycle and just before the kneading cycle begins, add the raisins to the dough.

5. At the end of the baking cycle, remove the bread promptly from the machine, taking care, as the oven surfaces will be very hot. Invert the bread pan onto a wire rack and shake several times to dislodge the bread. Allow to cool completely on the rack before slicing or wrapping for storage.

*R*um Raisin Bread

INGREDIENT	1-POUND LOAF	1¹/₂-POUND LOAF
Dark raisins	¹/₄ cup	¹/₃ cup
Dark rum	¹/₄ cup	¹/₃ cup
Whole wheat flour	2¹/₂ cups	3 cups
Dry milk	1 tablespoon	1 tablespoon
Grated lemon zest	2 teaspoons	1 tablespoon
Sea salt	1 teaspoon	1¹/₂ teaspoons
Toasted and chopped almonds	¹/₄ cup	¹/₃ cup
Toasted and chopped walnuts	¹/₄ cup	¹/₃ cup
Water	⁵/₈ cup	³/₄ cup plus 1 tablespoon
Egg(s), beaten	1 large	2 large
Canola, safflower, or sunflower oil	1 tablespoon	2 tablespoons
Active dry yeast	1 package	4 teaspoons

The rum adds a barely discernible flavor to this nutritious and luscious bread.

1. Place the raisins and rum in a small saucepan and bring to a boil. Remove from the heat and set aside to steep for 5 minutes. Drain the raisins and set aside to cool, reserving the liquid.

2. Fit the kneading blade firmly on the shaft in the bread pan. Carefully measure the flour, dry milk, lemon zest, salt, and nuts, and transfer to the pan. Add the reserved liquid, water, egg(s), oil, and yeast. Place the bread pan inside the machine and close the lid.

3. Program the breadmaker for the whole wheat mode. The unit will begin its operation.

4. At the end of the mixing cycle and just before the kneading cycle begins, add the drained raisins to the dough.

5. At the end of the baking cycle, remove the bread promptly from the machine, taking care, as the oven surfaces will be very hot. Invert the bread pan onto a wire rack and shake several times to dislodge the bread. Allow to cool completely on the rack before slicing or wrapping for storage.

Swedish Saffron Bread

INGREDIENT	1-POUND LOAF	1¹/₂-POUND LOAF
Bread flour	1¹/₄ cups	1¹/₂ cups
Whole wheat flour	³/₄ cup	1 cup
Oat-blend flour	¹/₂ cup	¹/₂ cup
Date sugar	2 tablespoons	3 tablespoons
Dry milk	1 tablespoon	1 tablespoon
Sea salt	1 teaspoon	1¹/₂ teaspoons
Saffron	4 threads	6 threads
Water	1 cup	1¹/₄ cups
Canola, safflower, or sunflower oil	1 tablespoon	2 tablespoons
Active dry yeast	1 package	4 teaspoons
Dried currants	¹/₂ cup	²/₃ cup

Currants lend a gentle sweetness and saffron adds color to this very Nordic loaf. It is especially nice slathered with cream cheese and topped with a spoonful of chutney.

1. Fit the kneading blade firmly on the shaft in the bread pan. Carefully measure the flours, sugar, dry milk, salt, and saffron, and transfer to the pan. Add the water, oil, and yeast. Place the bread pan inside the machine and close the lid.

2. Program the breadmaker for the whole wheat mode. The unit will begin its operation.

3. At the end of the mixing cycle and just before the kneading cycle begins, add the currants to the dough.

4. At the end of the baking cycle, remove the bread promptly from the machine, taking care, as the oven surfaces will be very hot. Invert the bread pan onto a wire rack and shake several times to dislodge the bread. Allow to cool completely on the rack before slicing or wrapping for storage.

Sweet Lemon Bread

INGREDIENT	1-POUND LOAF	1¹/₂-POUND LOAF
Whole wheat flour	$1^1/_4$ cups	$1^1/_2$ cups
Bread flour	1 cup	$1^1/_4$ cups
Brown rice flour	$^1/_4$ cup	$^1/_4$ cup
Dry milk	1 tablespoon	1 tablespoon
Grated lemon zest	2 teaspoons	1 tablespoon
Sea salt	1 teaspoon	$1^1/_2$ teaspoons
Water	$^5/_8$ cup	$^5/_8$ cup plus 1 tablespoon
Honey	$^1/_4$ cup	$^1/_4$ cup plus 1 tablespoon
Fresh lemon juice	2 tablespoons	3 tablespoons
Canola, safflower, or sunflower oil	2 tablespoons	3 tablespoons
Lemon extract	$^1/_2$ teaspoon	$^3/_4$ teaspoon
Active dry yeast	1 package	4 teaspoons

Serve this golden loaf with Lemon, Honey, and Walnut Cheese (page 273) and a bowl of fruit preserves for a wonderful treat at tea time.

1. Fit the kneading blade firmly on the shaft in the bread pan. Carefully measure the dry ingredients and transfer to the pan. Add the liquid ingredients and yeast. Place the bread pan inside the machine and close the lid.

2. Program the breadmaker for the whole wheat mode. The unit will begin its operation.

3. At the end of the baking cycle, remove the bread promptly from the machine, taking care, as the oven surfaces will be very hot. Invert the bread pan onto a wire rack and shake several times to dislodge the bread. Allow to cool completely on the rack before slicing or wrapping for storage.

$\mathcal{S}$hea's Apple Coffee Cake

INGREDIENT	1-POUND LOAF	1^{1}/$_{2}$-POUND LOAF
Milk	^{3}/$_{8}$ cup	^{1}/$_{2}$ cup
Bread flour	2^{1}/$_{4}$ cups	3 cups
Dry milk	2 tablespoons	3 tablespoons
Sea salt	1 teaspoon	1^{1}/$_{2}$ teaspoons
Water	^{1}/$_{2}$ cup	^{3}/$_{4}$ cup
Canola, safflower, or sunflower oil	2 tablespoons	3 tablespoons
Honey	1 tablespoon	2 tablespoons
Active dry yeast	2 teaspoons	1 package
Date sugar	^{1}/$_{3}$ cup	^{1}/$_{2}$ cup
Ground cinnamon	1^{1}/$_{2}$ teaspoons	2 teaspoons
Ground nutmeg	^{3}/$_{4}$ teaspoon	1 teaspoon
Grated orange zest	^{1}/$_{2}$ teaspoon	^{3}/$_{4}$ teaspoon
Granny Smith or other tart apples, peeled and sliced	2 large	3 large

*Try varying the fruit in this simple breakfast bread,
or filling it with a combination of fresh fruits.
It is especially luscious if you use fresh ripe peaches
and pitted Bing cherries.*

INGREDIENT	1-POUND LOAF	1¹/₂-POUND LOAF
Golden raisins	¹/₃ cup	¹/₂ cup
Softened soy margarine	3 tablespoons	¹/₄ cup
Egg, beaten	1 large	1 large

1. In a small saucepan, scald the milk by heating it just to the boiling point, and set aside to cool.

2. Fit the kneading blade firmly on the shaft in the bread pan. Carefully measure the flour, dry milk, and salt, and transfer to the pan. Add the cooled milk, water, oil, honey, and yeast. Place the bread pan inside the machine and close the lid.

3. Program the breadmaker for the white bread dough mode. The unit will begin its operation.

4. At the end of the rising cycle, turn the dough out onto a lightly floured surface. Cover the dough with a towel and let it rest for 10 minutes. In a small bowl, combine the sugar, cinnamon, nutmeg, and orange zest, and set aside.

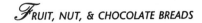

5. Roll the dough out into a large, $1/2$-inch-thick rectangle. Sprinkle the surface with a quarter of the sugar mixture, and place half of the apples down the center of the dough. Sprinkle the apples with half of the remaining sugar mixture and top with raisins. Arrange the remaining apples on top and sprinkle with the rest of the sugar mixture. Dot the apples with margarine.

6. Fold each of the long sides of dough over the apples, overlapping slightly in the middle. Pinch the dough together gently to seal well. Seal the ends in the same manner. Lightly oil a large baking sheet and carefully transfer the dough to the center. Cover loosely and set in a warm place for 30 minutes.

7. Brush the top of the bread with the beaten egg and bake in a preheated 400°F oven for 20 to 25 minutes, or until golden brown. Transfer to a wire rack and cool slightly. Can be served warm or cold.

CHAPTER 7

GRAIN & SEED BREADS

*L*earning about baking with whole grains is not as simple as it would seem. We have a multitude of readily available grains, varying according to species, processing techniques, and sources. Did you know there are over 200 varieties of barley alone? And they are not necessarily interchangeable—the species used for making beer is significantly different from the one we put into bread. The Glossary of Ingredients, beginning on page 12, describes, as simply as possible, the grains I use in this book.

There is quite a difference in the quality and taste of grains. The supermarket varieties are generally toasted, which adds to their shelf life but reduces the vitamin and mineral content. Any grain that is purchased whole and raw retains most of its nutrients. If you do not have a mill or a heavy-duty blender, you may be able to have your someone at local natural foods store grind the whole grains for you. When purchasing raw whole grains, take care that they have been stored covered and in a cool place to retain freshness. A number of growers and millers produce some very accept-

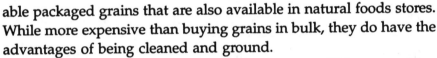

able packaged grains that are also available in natural foods stores. While more expensive than buying grains in bulk, they do have the advantages of being cleaned and ground.

If you purchase whole grains in bulk, you will have to clean them yourself. Rinse the grains twice and spread them out in a shallow pan to dry. Pick out any debris. Store the grains in a cool, dry place under airtight seals. If you have room in your refrigerator or freezer, store them there, especially during the summer months. Some grain products, such as wheat germ, contain oil that rapidly turns rancid at room temperature. But under refrigeration, they will keep for months.

Whole grain and seed breads have a hearty, aggressive flavor and consistency. They are composed of the very finest of our earth's natural harvest and provide a significant amount of nutrition and fiber in every slice. Once you become accustomed to their rich, chewy texture and aroma, other simple flour breads will pale in comparison. The breads in this chapter are compatible with many of the delectable whips, dips, spreads, and glazes in Chapter 10, beginning on page 271.

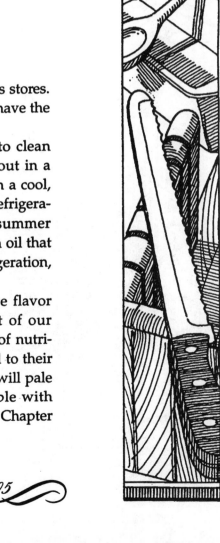

Anise Bread

INGREDIENT	1-POUND LOAF	1^1/$_2$-POUND LOAF
Whole wheat flour	1 cup	1^1/$_4$ cups
Brown rice flour	^{3}/$_4$ cup	1 cup
Bread flour	^{1}/$_2$ cup	^{1}/$_2$ cup
Gluten flour	^{1}/$_4$ cup	^{1}/$_4$ cup
Anise seeds	1 tablespoon	1^1/$_2$ tablespoons
Dry milk	1 tablespoon	1 tablespoon
Sea salt	1 teaspoon	1^1/$_2$ teaspoons
Water	1 cup	1^1/$_4$ cups
Canola, safflower, or sunflower oil	1 tablespoon	2 tablespoons
Honey	1 tablespoon	1^1/$_2$ tablespoons
Active dry yeast	1 package	4 teaspoons

You will find this crusty, light-colored loaf has the gentle aroma and flavor of anise seeds.

1. Fit the kneading blade firmly on the shaft in the bread pan. Carefully measure the dry ingredients and transfer to the pan. Add the liquid ingredients and yeast. Place the bread pan inside the machine and close the lid.

2. Program the breadmaker for the whole wheat mode. The unit will begin its operation.

3. At the end of the baking cycle, remove the bread promptly from the machine, taking care, as the oven surfaces will be very hot. Invert the bread pan onto a wire rack and shake several times to dislodge the bread. Allow to cool completely on the rack before slicing or wrapping for storage.

Cornmeal Bread

INGREDIENT	1-POUND LOAF	1^1/$_2$-POUND LOAF
Bread flour	1^1/$_2$ cups	1^2/$_3$ cups
Whole wheat flour	^{1}/$_2$ cup	^{2}/$_3$ cup
Yellow cornmeal	^{1}/$_2$ cup	^{2}/$_3$ cup
Dry milk	1 tablespoon	1 tablespoon
Sea salt	1 teaspoon	1^1/$_2$ teaspoons
Cayenne pepper	^{1}/$_2$ teaspoon, or to taste	1 teaspoon, or to taste
Water	^{2}/$_3$ cup	^{3}/$_4$ cup
Plain nonfat yogurt	^{1}/$_3$ cup	^{1}/$_2$ cup
Canola, safflower, or sunflower oil	1 tablespoon	2 tablespoons
Honey	1 tablespoon	2 tablespoons
Active dry yeast	2 teaspoons	1 package

This is the perfect bread to serve with a big wedge of sharp Cheddar cheese and a steaming, fragrant bowl of hot chili.

1. Fit the kneading blade firmly on the shaft in the bread pan. Carefully measure the dry ingredients and transfer to the pan. Add the liquid ingredients and yeast. Place the bread pan inside the machine and close the lid.

2. Program the breadmaker for the whole wheat mode. The unit will begin its operation.

3. At the end of the baking cycle, remove the bread promptly from the machine, taking care, as the oven surfaces will be very hot. Invert the bread pan onto a wire rack and shake several times to dislodge the bread. Allow to cool completely on the rack before slicing or wrapping for storage.

Lemon Poppy Bread

INGREDIENT	1-POUND LOAF	1¹/₂-POUND LOAF
Skim milk	¹/₂ cup	¹/₂ cup
Whole wheat flour	1³/₄ cups	2 cups
Bread flour	¹/₂ cup	²/₃ cup
Oat bran	¹/₄ cup	¹/₃ cup
Grated lemon zest	2 tablespoons	3 tablespoons
Poppy seeds	2 tablespoons	3 tablespoons
Dry milk	1 tablespoon	1 tablespoon
Sea salt	1 teaspoon	1¹/₂ teaspoons
Water	¹/₂ cup	³/₄ cup
Honey	2 tablespoons	3 tablespoons
Canola, safflower, or sunflower oil	1 tablespoon	1¹/₂ tablespoons
Active dry yeast	1 package	4 teaspoons

I often make this lemony, poppy seed bread when I plan to serve stuffed cabbage. It seems to fit right in with any Hungarian-style dish.

1. In a small saucepan, scald the milk by heating it just to the boiling point, and set aside to cool.

2. Fit the kneading blade firmly on the shaft in the bread pan. Carefully measure the dry ingredients and transfer to the pan. Add the cooled milk, water, honey, oil, and yeast. Place the bread pan inside the machine and close the lid.

3. Program the breadmaker for the whole wheat mode. The unit will begin its operation.

4. At the end of the baking cycle, remove the bread promptly from the machine, taking care, as the oven surfaces will be very hot. Invert the bread pan onto a wire rack and shake several times to dislodge the bread. Allow to cool completely on the rack before slicing or wrapping for storage.

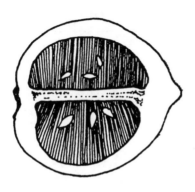

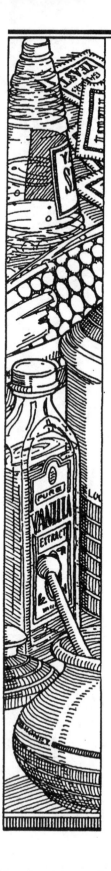

Multi-Grain Almond Bread

INGREDIENT	1-POUND LOAF	1¹/₂-POUND LOAF
Whole wheat flour	2 cups	2¹/₄ cups
Toasted and finely chopped almonds	3 tablespoons	¹/₄ cup
Graham flour	2 tablespoons	3 tablespoons
Bran cereal	2 tablespoons	3 tablespoons
Rolled oats	2 tablespoons	3 tablespoons
Gluten flour	1¹/₂ tablespoons	2 tablespoons
Whole rye flour	1 tablespoon	2 tablespoons
Brown rice flour	1 tablespoon	1 tablespoon
Dry milk	1 tablespoon	1 tablespoon
Yellow cornmeal	1 teaspoon	2 teaspoons
Sea salt	1 teaspoon	1¹/₂ teaspoons
Water	1 cup	1¹/₄ cups
Canola, safflower, or sunflower oil	1 tablespoon	2 tablespoons
Honey	1 tablespoon	2 tablespoons
Almond extract	1 teaspoon	1 teaspoon
Active dry yeast	1 package	4 teaspoons

This highly nutritious bread makes absolutely fantastic sandwiches. Try avocado slices, shredded cheese, crisp sprouts, and a creamy herb dressing between slices of this nutty bread.

1. Fit the kneading blade firmly on the shaft in the bread pan. Carefully measure the dry ingredients and transfer to the pan. Add the liquid ingredients and yeast. Place the bread pan inside the machine and close the lid.

2. Program the breadmaker for the whole wheat mode. The unit will begin its operation.

3. At the end of the baking cycle, remove the bread promptly from the machine, taking care, as the oven surfaces will be very hot. Invert the bread pan onto a wire rack and shake several times to dislodge the bread. Allow to cool completely on the rack before slicing or wrapping for storage.

Six-Grain Bread

INGREDIENT	1-POUND LOAF	1 1/2-POUND LOAF
Whole wheat flour	1 cup	1 cup plus 2 tablespoons
Whole rye flour	1 cup	1 cup plus 2 tablespoons
Gluten flour	1/4 cup	1/4 cup plus 2 tablespoons
Toasted and coarsely ground almonds	3 tablespoons	1/4 cup
Date sugar	2 tablespoons	3 tablespoons
Sunflower seeds	2 tablespoons	3 tablespoons
Rolled oats	1 tablespoon	2 tablespoons
Bran cereal	1 tablespoon	2 tablespoons
Soy flakes	1 tablespoon	2 tablespoons
Wheat germ	1 tablespoon	2 tablespoons
Dry milk	1 tablespoon	2 tablespoons
Ground cumin	1 tablespoon	1 1/2 tablespoons
Sea salt	1 teaspoon	1 1/2 teaspoons

*Hearty and nourishing, you will find this great loaf
has the distinctive flavor of cumin.
It is one of my favorite breads.*

INGREDIENT	1-POUND LOAF	1¹/₂-POUND LOAF
Water	1 cup	1¹/₄ cups
Canola, safflower, or sunflower oil	1 tablespoon	2 tablespoons
Molasses	1 tablespoon	2 tablespoons
Active dry yeast	1 package	4 teaspoons

1. Fit the kneading blade firmly on the shaft in the bread pan. Carefully measure the dry ingredients and transfer to the pan. Add the liquid ingredients and yeast. Place the bread pan inside the machine and close the lid.

2. Program the breadmaker for the whole wheat mode. The unit will begin its operation.

3. At the end of the baking cycle, remove the bread promptly from the machine, taking care, as the oven surfaces will be very hot. Invert the bread pan onto a wire rack and shake several times to dislodge the bread. Allow to cool completely on the rack before slicing or wrapping for storage.

$\mathcal{S}$ix-Seed Bread

INGREDIENT	1-POUND LOAF	1^1/$_2$-POUND LOAF
Whole wheat flour	1^1/$_4$ cups	1^1/$_2$ cups
Bread flour	1 cup	1^1/$_4$ cups
Toasted and chopped walnuts	^{1}/$_2$ cup	^{2}/$_3$ cup
Yellow cornmeal	2 tablespoons	2 tablespoons
Gluten flour	1 tablespoon	2 tablespoons
Date sugar	1 tablespoon	2 tablespoons
Dry milk	1 tablespoon	1^1/$_2$ tablespoons
Minced fresh rosemary, or dried rosemary	1 tablespoon 1 teaspoon	1^1/$_2$ tablespoons 1 tablespoon
Celery seeds	2 teaspoons	1 tablespoon
Poppy seeds	2 teaspoons	2 teaspoons
Sesame seeds	1 teaspoon	2 teaspoons
Anise seeds	1 teaspoon	2 teaspoons
Fennel seeds	1 teaspoon	2 teaspoons
Caraway seeds	1 teaspoon	2 teaspoons

Top Left and Center: Chocolate Chip and Nut Bread (page 164) With Maple Cream (page 292)
Top Right: Orange Raisin Bread (page 184)
Bottom: Banana Date Bread (page 160)

Top Left: Jalapeno Cheese Bread (page 146)
Center: Fiesta Bread (page 50)
Bottom: Gazpacho Bread (page 228)

Such a perfect bread—filled with a variety of interesting flavors and textures—that you will end up making it again and again.

INGREDIENT	1-POUND LOAF	1¹/₂-POUND LOAF
Sea salt	1 teaspoon	1¹/₂ teaspoons
Water	1 cup	1¹/₄ cups
Canola, safflower, or sunflower oil	1 tablespoon	2 tablespoons
Active dry yeast	1 package	4 teaspoons

1. Fit the kneading blade firmly on the shaft in the bread pan. Carefully measure the dry ingredients and transfer to the pan. Add the liquid ingredients and yeast. Place the bread pan inside the machine and close the lid.

2. Program the breadmaker for the whole wheat mode. The unit will begin its operation.

3. At the end of the baking cycle, remove the bread promptly from the machine, taking care, as the oven surfaces will be very hot. Invert the bread pan onto a wire rack and shake several times to dislodge the bread. Allow to cool completely on the rack before slicing or wrapping for storage.

*N*ine-Grain Bread

INGREDIENT	1-POUND LOAF	1¹/2-POUND LOAF
Whole wheat flour	1 cup	1^1/$_4$ cups
Bread flour	^{1}/$_2$ cup	^{2}/$_3$ cup
Whole rye flour	^{1}/$_4$ cup	^{1}/$_3$ cup
Gluten flour	^{1}/$_4$ cup	^{1}/$_3$ cup
Buckwheat flour	2 tablespoons	3 tablespoons
Sunflower seeds	2 tablespoons	3 tablespoons
Wheat germ	2 tablespoons	2 tablespoons
Oat-blend flour	1 tablespoon	2 tablespoons
Bran cereal	1 tablespoon	2 tablespoons
Popcorn flour	1 tablespoon	2 tablespoons
Rolled oats	1 tablespoon	2 tablespoons
Dry milk	1 tablespoon	2 tablespoons
Yellow cornmeal	1 tablespoon	1 tablespoon
Sea salt	1 teaspoon	1^1/$_2$ teaspoons
Water	1 cup	1^1/$_4$ cups

*This flavorful bread is a powerhouse of nutrition
and makes terrific sandwiches.*

INGREDIENT	1-POUND LOAF	1¹/₂-POUND LOAF
Canola, safflower, or sunflower oil	2 tablespoons	3 tablespoons
Honey	2 tablespoons	3 tablespoons
Active dry yeast	1 package	4 teaspoons

1. Fit the kneading blade firmly on the shaft in the bread pan. Carefully measure the dry ingredients and transfer to the pan. Add the liquid ingredients and the yeast. Place the bread pan inside the machine and close the lid.

2. Program the breadmaker for the whole wheat mode. The unit will begin its operation.

3. At the end of the baking cycle, remove the bread promptly from the machine, taking care, as the oven surfaces will be very hot. Invert the bread pan onto a wire rack and shake several times to dislodge the bread. Allow to cool completely on the rack before slicing or wrapping for storage.

 VEGETABLE BREADS

There are few whole grain breads that are as nutritious as those filled with vegetables. And there is no time of day that one of these breads cannot be eaten. Sweet carrot and raisin bread for breakfast, slices of zucchini bread filled with crisp vegetables and a creamy cheese for lunch, or a hot loaf of olive and mint bread served alongside a Greek moussaka for dinner—all fit a daily menu.

Incorporating vegetables into your breads requires special attention to the proportion of dry to liquid ingredients. When you are baking bread by hand, you have the opportunity to feel the dough and become aware of any problems in its consistency before it is baked. This, of course, is not possible with a breadmaker. So when you add ingredients to bread dough, particularly when the ingredients, such as vegetables, contain water, you must take care to maintain the proper proportion of flour to water.

The recipes in this chapter reflect many hours of experimentation

to ensure that each vegetable bread you create comes out light, savory, and just moist enough. But vegetables vary considerably in their water content. I've found tomatoes and squashes, in particular, to be consistently inconsistent. To compensate for these irregularities, I suggest you do two things: First, when adding any vegetable to a bread dough, chop or mince it as directed, then spread it out on a double thickness of paper towels to dry. Let the towels absorb the excess liquid for at least 10 minutes, changing the towels if they become too wet. Second, add the vegetables near the end of the mixing cycle and before the kneading begins. This way, the vegetables will not have the opportunity to release too much of their moisture.

I hope you will use these recipes as a starting point for creating your own vegetable breads. Begin with my basic proportions of dry to liquid ingredients and simply substitute your own choice of vegetables, herbs, and spices. Good baking and good eating!

Carrot Raisin Bread

INGREDIENT	1-POUND LOAF	1½-POUND LOAF
Whole wheat flour	1¼ cups	1⅓ cups
Bread flour	1 cup	1⅓ cups
Gluten flour	1 tablespoon	2 tablespoons
Rolled oats	¼ cup	⅓ cup
Dry milk	1 tablespoon	1 tablespoon
Sea salt	1 teaspoon	1½ teaspoons
Ground mace	½ teaspoon	1 teaspoon
Water	1 cup	1¼ cups
Honey	2 tablespoons	3 tablespoons
Canola, safflower, or sunflower oil	1 tablespoon	2 tablespoons
Active dry yeast	1 package	4 teaspoons
Scraped and shredded carrot	⅔ cup, loosely packed	1 cup, loosely packed
Dark raisins	¼ cup	⅓ cup

Experiment using this bread for sandwiches, particularly with cream cheese and vegetable fillings.

1. Fit the kneading blade firmly on the shaft in the bread pan. Carefully measure the flours, oats, dry milk, salt, and mace, and transfer to the pan. Add the water, honey, oil, and yeast. Place the bread pan inside the machine and close the lid.

2. Program the breadmaker for the whole wheat mode. The unit will begin its operation.

3. At the end of the mixing cycle and just before the kneading cycle begins, add the carrots and raisins to the dough.

4. At the end of the baking cycle, remove the bread promptly from the machine, taking care, as the oven surfaces will be very hot. Invert the bread pan onto a wire rack and shake several times to dislodge the bread. Allow to cool completely on the rack before slicing or wrapping for storage.

Crusty Corn Bread

INGREDIENT	1-POUND LOAF	1¹/₂-POUND LOAF
Whole wheat flour	2 cups	2¹/₃ cups
Gluten flour	¹/₄ cup	¹/₃ cup
Yellow cornmeal	¹/₄ cup	¹/₃ cup
Dry milk	1 tablespoon	1 tablespoon
Date sugar	1 tablespoon	2 tablespoons
Grated orange zest	1 tablespoon	2 tablespoons
Sea salt	1 teaspoon	1¹/₂ teaspoons
Crushed dried hot red chilies	¹/₂ teaspoon or to taste	1 teaspoon or to taste
Water	1 cup	1¹/₄ cups
Canola, safflower, or sunflower oil	2 tablespoons	3 tablespoons
Honey	1 tablespoon	2 tablespoons
Active dry yeast	1 package	4 teaspoons
Fresh corn kernels, drained well	¹/₄ cup	¹/₃ cup

A very savory bread that is perfect with Mexican-style meals, this loaf has a crunchy, tasty crust.

1. Fit the kneading blade firmly on the shaft in the bread pan. Carefully measure the flours, cornmeal, sugar, orange zest, salt, and chilies, and transfer to the pan. Add the water, oil, honey, and yeast. Place the bread pan inside the machine and close the lid.

2. Program the breadmaker for the whole wheat mode. The unit will begin its operation.

3. At the end of the mixing cycle and just before the kneading cycle begins, add the corn kernels to the dough.

4. At the end of the baking cycle, remove the bread promptly from the machine, taking care, as the oven surfaces will be very hot. Invert the bread pan onto a wire rack and shake several times to dislodge the bread. Allow to cool completely on the rack before slicing or wrapping for storage.

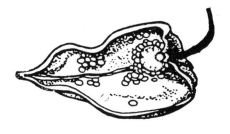

French Onion Bread

INGREDIENT	1-POUND LOAF	1¹/₂-POUND LOAF
Bread flour	2^1/$_4$ cups	3 cups
Dry onion soup mix	1 package (1 ounce)	1^1/$_3$ packages
Date sugar	3 tablespoons	^{1}/$_4$ cup
Crushed garlic	1 clove	2 cloves
Scallions (including 1 inch of green tops), minced	4	5
Sea salt	^{1}/$_2$ teaspoon	1 teaspoon
Water	^{7}/$_8$ cup	1^1/$_4$ cups
Canola, safflower, or sunflower oil	2 tablespoons	3 tablespoons
Active dry yeast	2 teaspoons	1 package
Cubed Emmenthaler or Swiss cheese	1 cup	1^1/$_2$ cups

This bread is reminiscent of the hot, steamy French onion soup I enjoyed in Paris—even down to the cheese.

1. Fit the kneading blade firmly on the shaft in the bread pan. Carefully measure the flour, soup mix, sugar, garlic, scallions, and sea salt, and transfer to the pan. Add the water, oil, and yeast. Place the bread pan inside the machine and close the lid.

2. Program the breadmaker for the whole wheat mode. The unit will begin its operation.

3. At the end of the mixing cycle and just before the kneading cycle begins, add the cheese to the dough.

4. At the end of the baking cycle, remove the bread promptly from the machine, taking care, as the oven surfaces will be very hot. Invert the bread pan onto a wire rack and shake several times to dislodge the bread. Allow to cool completely on the rack before slicing or wrapping for storage.

Gazpacho Bread

INGREDIENT	1-POUND LOAF	1^1/$_2$-POUND LOAF
Whole wheat flour	1^1/$_2$ cups	1^3/$_4$ cups
Bread flour	^{3}/$_4$ cup	1 cup
Gluten flour	^{1}/$_4$ cup	^{1}/$_4$ cup
Date sugar	2 tablespoons	3 tablespoons
Sea salt	^{1}/$_4$ teaspoon	^{1}/$_2$ teaspoon
Water	^{1}/$_2$ cup	^{3}/$_4$ cup
Bloody Mary mix, tomato juice, or V-8 juice	^{1}/$_2$ cup	^{1}/$_2$ cup
Olive oil	1 tablespoon	2 tablespoons
Active dry yeast	1 package	4 teaspoons
Minced sweet yellow onion	3 tablespoons	^{1}/$_4$ cup
Green bell pepper, seeded and minced	2 tablespoons	3 tablespoons
Ripe tomato, seeded, chopped, and drained well	1 medium	1 large

 THE BREAD MACHINE GOURMET

An ideal brunch bread, this rosy loaf has terrific tang and is filled with loads of vegetables. For added zip, use a spicy Bloody Mary mix.

1. Fit the kneading blade firmly on the shaft in the bread pan. Carefully measure the flours, sugar, and sea salt, and transfer to the pan. Add the water, Bloody Mary mix, oil, and yeast. Place the bread pan inside the machine and close the lid.

2. Program the breadmaker for the whole wheat mode. The unit will begin its operation.

3. At the end of the mixing cycle and just before the kneading cycle begins, add the onion, pepper, and tomato to the dough.

4. At the end of the baking cycle, remove the bread promptly from the machine, taking care, as the oven surfaces will be very hot. Invert the bread pan onto a wire rack and shake several times to dislodge the bread. Allow to cool completely on the rack before slicing or wrapping for storage.

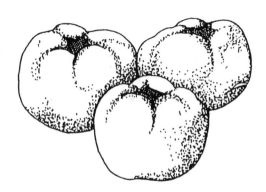

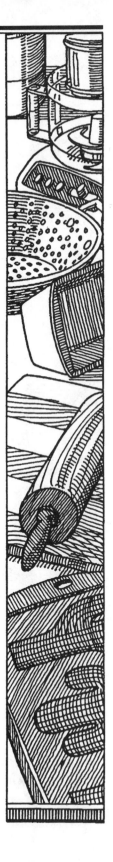

$\mathcal{O}$live and Mint Bread

INGREDIENT	1-POUND LOAF	1½-POUND LOAF
Whole wheat flour	1¼ cups	1½ cups
Bread flour	1¼ cups	1½ cups
Minced fresh mint, or dried mint	1 tablespoon 1 teaspoon	2 tablespoons 1 teaspoon
Minced fresh basil, or dried basil	1 teaspoon ½ teaspoon	2 teaspoons 1 teaspoon
Sea salt	1 teaspoon	1½ teaspoons
Water	1 cup	1¼ cups
Olive oil	1 tablespoon	2 tablespoons
Honey	1 teaspoon	2 teaspoons
Active dry yeast	1 package	4 teaspoons
Pitted, drained, and minced Spanish green olives	⅓ cup	½ cup

THE BREAD MACHINE GOURMET

Delectable and moist are two adjectives that best describe this unique bread, which is one of my family's favorites.

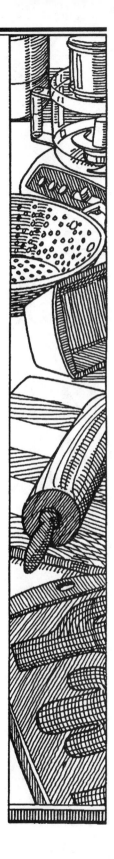

1. Fit the kneading blade firmly on the shaft in the bread pan. Carefully measure the flours, mint, basil, and salt, and transfer to the pan. Add the water, oil, honey, and yeast. Place the bread pan inside the machine and close the lid.

2. Program the breadmaker for the whole wheat mode. The unit will begin its operation.

3. At the end of the mixing cycle and just before the kneading cycle begins, add the olives to the dough.

4. At the end of the baking cycle, remove the bread promptly from the machine, taking care, as the oven surfaces will be very hot. Invert the bread pan onto a wire rack and shake several times to dislodge the bread. Allow to cool completely on the rack before slicing or wrapping for storage.

VEGETABLE BREADS

Onion Bread Sticks

INGREDIENT	1-POUND LOAF	1^1/$_2$-POUND LOAF
Milk	^{3}/$_4$ cup	1 cup
Whole wheat flour	1^1/$_4$ cups	1^1/$_2$ cups
Bread flour	1 cup	1^1/$_4$ cups
Brown rice flour	^{1}/$_4$ cup	^{1}/$_4$ cup
Sea salt	1 teaspoon	1^1/$_2$ teaspoons
Celery seeds	^{1}/$_2$ teaspoon	1 teaspoon
Sage	^{1}/$_4$ teaspoon	^{1}/$_2$ teaspoon
Honey	2 tablespoons	3 tablespoons
Olive oil	1 tablespoon	2 tablespoons
Active dry yeast	1 package	4 teaspoons
Chopped sweet yellow onion	1 cup (about 1 medium onion)	1^1/$_4$ cups (about 1 medium onion)
Egg white(s), beaten until frothy	1	2
Coarse sea salt	2 tablespoons	3 tablespoons

This bread can also be baked in the breadmaker, although I prefer forming the dough into bread sticks, sprinkling them with sea salt, and baking them in the oven.

1. In a small saucepan, scald the milk by heating it just to the boiling point, and remove from the heat. Set aside to cool.

2. Fit the kneading blade firmly on the shaft in the bread pan. Carefully measure the flours, salt, celery seeds, and sage, and transfer to the pan. Add the cooled milk, honey, oil, and yeast. Place the bread pan inside the machine and close the lid.

3. Program the breadmaker for the whole wheat dough mode. The unit will begin its operation.

4. At the end of the mixing cycle and just before kneading begins, add the onions to the dough.

5. At the end of the rising cycle, turn the dough out onto a lightly floured surface. Cover and allow the dough to rest for 10 minutes. Divide the dough into 6 (or 9) pieces. With floured hands, roll each piece into an 8-inch long stick. Lightly oil a large baking sheet and arrange the sticks on the sheet, spacing them 1-inch apart. Lightly cover and set it in a warm place for 20 minutes.

6. Lightly brush the tops of the sticks with beaten egg white and sprinkle with coarse sea salt. Bake the bread sticks in a preheated 375°F oven for 10 to 12 minutes until golden. Serve warm or allow to cool completely on a rack before wrapping for storage. Makes 6 (or 9) bread sticks.

 VEGETABLE BREADS

$\mathcal{P}$otato Dill Bread

INGREDIENT	1-POUND LOAF	1½-POUND LOAF
Whole wheat flour	1 cup	1 cup plus 3 tablespoons
Bread flour	1 cup	1 cup plus 2 tablespoons
Brown rice flour	6 tablespoons	½ cup
Gluten flour	3 tablespoons	¼ cup
Snipped fresh dill, or dried dillweed	3 tablespoons 1 tablespoon	¼ cup 2 tablespoons
Dry milk	2 tablespoons	3 tablespoons
Crushed garlic	1 clove	2 cloves
Sea salt	1 teaspoon	1½ teaspoons
Beer, flat and at room temperature	1 cup	1¼ cups
Canola, safflower, or sunflower oil	1 tablespoon	2 tablespoons
Honey	1 teaspoon	2 teaspoons
Active dry yeast	1 package	4 teaspoons
Mashed potatoes	½ cup (about 1 small potato)	⅔ cup (about 1 small potato)

This high and light loaf with its unassuming flavor fits well in any menu.

1. Fit the kneading blade firmly on the shaft in the bread pan. Carefully measure the dry ingredients and transfer to the pan. Add the beer, oil, honey, and yeast. Place the bread pan inside the machine and close the lid.

2. Program the breadmaker for the whole wheat mode. The unit will begin its operation.

3. At the end of the mixing cycle and just before the kneading cycle begins, add the potatoes to the dough.

4. At the end of the baking cycle, remove the bread promptly from the machine, taking care, as the oven surfaces will be very hot. Invert the bread pan onto a wire rack and shake several times to dislodge the bread. Allow to cool completely on the rack before slicing or wrapping for storage.

$\mathscr{P}$umpkin Bread

INGREDIENT	1-POUND LOAF	1½-POUND LOAF
Whole wheat flour	1½ cups	1¾ cups
Bread flour	1 cup	1¼ cups
Dry milk	1 tablespoon	2 tablespoons
Sea salt	1 teaspoon	1½ teaspoons
Pumpkin pie spice	1 teaspoon	1½ teaspoons
Grated orange zest	1 teaspoon	2 teaspoons
Water	½ cup	½ cup
Fresh orange juice	5 tablespoons	½ cup
Canola, safflower, or sunflower oil	1 tablespoon	2 tablespoons
Honey	1 tablespoon	1 tablespoon
Active dry yeast	1 package	4 teaspoons
Mashed pumpkin (fresh or canned)	½ cup	⅔ cup
Golden raisins	¼ cup	⅓ cup

THE BREAD MACHINE GOURMET

I love the rich, golden-orange color of this loaf with its airy, light sweetness. Just perfect for breakfast.

1. Fit the kneading blade firmly on the shaft in the bread pan. Carefully measure the dry ingredients and transfer to the pan. Add the water, orange juice, oil, honey, and yeast. Place the bread pan inside the machine and close the lid.

2. Program the breadmaker for the whole wheat mode. The unit will begin its operation.

3. At the end of the mixing cycle and just before the kneading cycle begins, add the pumpkin and raisins to the dough.

4. At the end of the baking cycle, remove the bread promptly from the machine, taking care, as the oven surfaces will be very hot. Invert the bread pan onto a wire rack and shake several times to dislodge the bread. Allow to cool completely on the rack before slicing or wrapping for storage.

Spinach Feta Bread

INGREDIENT	1-POUND LOAF	1¹/₂-POUND LOAF
Whole wheat flour	1¹/₄ cups	1¹/₂ cups
Bread flour	1¹/₄ cups	1¹/₂ cups
Snipped fresh dill, or dried dillweed	2 tablespoons 1 tablespoon	3 tablespoons 4 teaspoons
Sea salt	1 teaspoon	1¹/₂ teaspoons
Date sugar	1 teaspoon	1¹/₂ teaspoons
Water	1 cup	1¹/₄ cups
Olive oil	3 tablespoons	¹/₄ cup
Active dry yeast	1 package	4 teaspoons
Fresh spinach, or frozen spinach (thawed), chopped	16 ounces 1 package (10 ounces)	20 ounces 1¹/₂ packages
Crumbled feta cheese	³/₄ cup	1¹/₄ cups
Shredded mozzarella cheese	³/₄ cup	1¹/₄ cups
Part-skim ricotta cheese	¹/₂ cup	³/₄ cup
Crushed garlic	1 clove	2 cloves
Black pepper	¹/₂ teaspoon	1 teaspoon
Egg, beaten	1 large	1 large

My first attempt at a spinach feta bread resulted in a green-colored loaf with a spinach flavor so intense you couldn't taste the cheese. Now, I fold the spinach and feta into the dough just before baking. It's wonderful!

---

1. Fit the kneading blade firmly on the shaft in the bread pan. Carefully measure the flours, dill, salt, and sugar, and transfer to the pan. Add the water, 1 tablespoon (or 2 tablespoons) olive oil, and the yeast. Place the bread pan inside the machine and close the lid.

---

2. Program the breadmaker for the whole wheat dough mode. The unit will begin its operation.

---

3. At the end of the rising cycle, turn the dough out onto a lightly floured surface. Cover and allow to rest for 10 minutes. Meanwhile, in a medium bowl, combine the spinach (squeezed dry), the feta, mozzarella, and ricotta cheeses, the rest of the olive oil, the garlic, and black pepper. Mix together thoroughly.

---

4. With a floured rolling pin, roll the dough out to a 1/2-inch-thick rectangle. Spread the spinach mixture over the dough to within 1/2 inch of the edges. Starting at one of the long ends, roll the dough into a log, pinching the ends together.

---

5. Lightly oil a baking sheet. Arrange the log, seam side down, in the middle of the sheet. Cover and set in a warm place for 20 minutes. Lightly brush the loaf with the beaten egg and bake in a preheated 425°F oven for 20 minutes or until golden. Transfer to a wire rack and allow to cool for 10 minutes before slicing and serving.

Sweet Potato Corn Muffins

INGREDIENT	1-POUND LOAF	1$\frac{1}{2}$-POUND LOAF
Water	1 cup	1$\frac{1}{4}$ cups
Yellow cornmeal	1 cup	1$\frac{1}{4}$ cups
Bread flour	1$\frac{1}{2}$ cups	1$\frac{3}{4}$ cups
Dry milk	1 tablespoon	2 tablespoons
Sea salt	1 teaspoon	1$\frac{1}{2}$ teaspoons
Mashed sweet potato	$\frac{1}{2}$ cup (about 1 small sweet potato)	$\frac{2}{3}$ cup (about 1 small sweet potato)
Canola, safflower, or sunflower oil	2 tablespoons	3 tablespoons
Honey	2 tablespoons	3 tablespoons
Active dry yeast	1 package	4 teaspoons

The potato and honey add a gentle sweetness,
and the cornmeal provides the fiber
in these easily prepared muffins.

1. In a small saucepan, bring the water to a boil. Place the cornmeal in a medium bowl and cover with the boiling water. Stir once and allow to sit for 20 minutes until cool.

2. Fit the kneading blade firmly on the shaft in the bread pan. Carefully measure the flour, milk, and salt, and transfer to the pan. Add the cooled cornmeal, sweet potato, oil, honey, and yeast. Place the bread pan inside the machine and close the lid.

3. Program the breadmaker for the white bread dough mode. The unit will begin its operation.

4. Lightly oil 6 (or 9) large muffin cups and set aside. At the end of the rising cycle, turn the dough out onto a lightly floured surface. Divide the dough into 6 (or 9) pieces and place each in one of the muffin cups. Cover lightly and set in a warm place for 30 minutes.

5. Bake the muffins in a preheated 400°F oven for 25 to 30 minutes until golden. Transfer to a wire rack and allow to cool slightly before serving. Makes 6 (or 9) muffins.

Vegetable Soup Bread

INGREDIENT	1-POUND LOAF	1^1/$_2$-POUND LOAF
Dehydrated vegetable soup mix	1 package (1 ounce)	1^1/$_2$ packages
Boiling water	1 cup	1^1/$_4$ cups
Whole wheat flour	2 cups	2^1/$_4$ cups
Bread flour	^{1}/$_2$ cup	^{3}/$_4$ cup
Dry milk	1 tablespoon	1 tablespoon
Olive oil	1 tablespoon	1^1/$_2$ tablespoons
Honey	1 tablespoon	1^1/$_2$ tablespoons
Active dry yeast	1 package	4 teaspoons

For a more subtly flavored bread, halve the soup-mix ingredient called for in this recipe.

1. Place the soup mix in a small bowl and cover with boiling water. Let it stand until cool.

2. Fit the kneading blade firmly on the shaft in the bread pan. Carefully measure the dry ingredients and transfer to the pan. Add the cooled soup, oil, honey, and yeast. Place the bread pan inside the machine and close the lid.

3. Program the breadmaker for the whole wheat mode. The unit will begin its operation.

4. At the end of the baking cycle, remove the bread promptly from the machine, taking care, as the oven surfaces will be very hot. Invert the bread pan onto a wire rack and shake several times to dislodge the bread. Allow to cool completely on the rack before slicing or wrapping for storage.

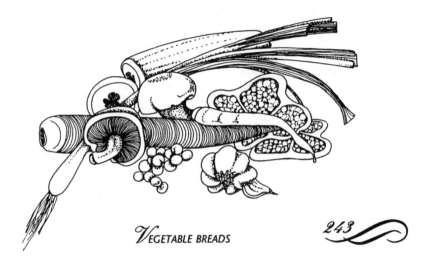

Vegetable Breads

243

CHAPTER 9

HOLIDAY BREADS & SWEET ROLLS

*T*here are so many customs connected with our holidays—from the rituals of our ancestors to the new traditions we begin even today. Many of these customs revolve around the preparation and enjoyment of food. Sharing food has always been a part of family, friendship, and hospitality. When I think of the holidays, I think of food. I anticipate the wonderful tastes and aromas, long before the decorations appear in the stores.

Perhaps no other foods are connected more with holidays and traditions than those we bake. Preparing special breads, rolls, and buns as our grandmothers and their grandmothers did, causes us to remember the times when we were wild with anticipation of an approaching celebration, and feeling very loved by those around us. Is it any wonder that we try to reproduce these feelings for our families?

In this chapter, I have included my versions of favorite holiday breads from around the world (many of which can be easily decorated or topped with one of the glazes found in Chapter 10). For all of these recipes, the breadmaker kneads the dough and allows it to rise. Once it's risen, you can shape the bread by hand and bake it in a conventional oven. Also included in this chapter are a number of sweet roll recipes that are perfect to enjoy at breadfast or tea time.

I hope the recipes in this chapter help you recall the warm, loving holidays of your past and put you in the mood for the holidays of your future.

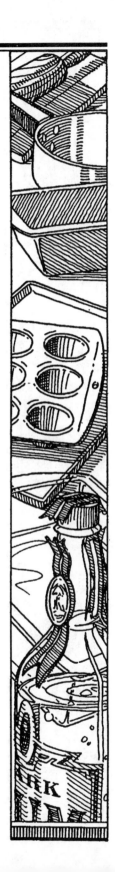

Cinnamon Buns

INGREDIENT	1-POUND LOAF	1^1/$_2$-POUND LOAF
Bread flour	1^1/$_2$ cups	1^3/$_4$ cups
Whole wheat flour	1 cup	1^1/$_4$ cups
Date sugar	3 tablespoons	^{1}/$_4$ cup
Dry milk	1 tablespoon	1^1/$_2$ tablespoons
Sea salt	1 teaspoon	1^1/$_2$ teaspoons
Ground nutmeg	^{1}/$_2$ teaspoon	1 teaspoon
Water	1 cup	1^1/$_4$ cups
Canola, safflower, or sunflower oil	1 tablespoon	2 tablespoons
Active dry yeast	1 package	4 teaspoons
Toasted rolled oats	1 cup	1^1/$_3$ cups
Melted soy margarine	^{1}/$_3$ cup	^{1}/$_2$ cup
Honey	^{1}/$_4$ cup	^{1}/$_3$ cup
Golden raisins	2 tablespoons	3 tablespoons
Ground cinnamon	2 teaspoons	1 tablespoon

THE BREAD MACHINE GOURMET

Enjoy these luscious cinnamon buns, which are surprisingly low in fat and calories.

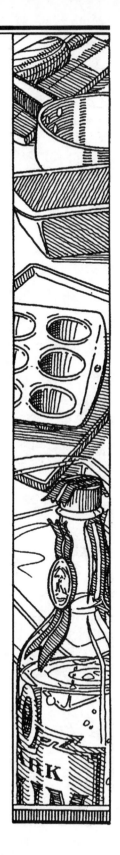

1. Fit the kneading blade firmly on the shaft in the bread pan. Carefully measure the flours, sugar, dry milk, salt, and nutmeg, and transfer to the pan. Add the water, oil, and yeast. Place the bread pan inside the machine and close the lid.

2. Program the breadmaker for the whole wheat dough mode. The unit will begin its operation.

3. At the end of the rising cycle, turn the dough out onto a lightly floured surface. Cover and let rest 10 minutes. Meanwhile, lightly oil an 8-inch (or 9-inch) square baking pan.

4. In a small bowl, with a wooden spoon, combine the oats, margarine, honey, raisins, and cinnamon. With a floured rolling pin, roll the dough into a large, 1/2-inch-thick rectangle. Evenly spread the oat mixture to within 1/2 inch of the sides.

5. Starting from one of the long sides, roll the dough up tightly, pinching the ends together gently. With a sharp knife, slice into 2-inch pieces and place on end in the pan. Cover loosely, and set in a warm place for 30 minutes.

6. Bake the rolls in a preheated 350°F oven for 35 to 40 minutes or until golden. If you wish, spread the rolls with a glaze while they are still warm. Makes 9 (or 12) cinnamon buns.

Easter Buns

INGREDIENT	1-POUND LOAF	1¹/2-POUND LOAF
Milk	1/2 cup	1/2 cup
Whole wheat flour	2 cups	2¹/4 cups
Bread flour	1/2 cup	3/4 cup
Minced candied citron	1/2 cup	2/3 cup
Date sugar	1/4 cup	1/3 cup
Dry milk	1 tablespoon	1¹/2 tablespoons
Sea salt	1 teaspoon	1¹/2 teaspoons
Ground nutmeg	1/2 teaspoon	3/4 teaspoon
Soy margarine	1/4 cup	1/3 cup
Water	1/2 cup	3/4 cup
Active dry yeast	1 package	4 teaspoons
Sifted confectioners' sugar	1/2 cup	1/2 cup
Egg white(s), beaten until frothy	1	2
Chopped candied cherries	1/2 cup	3/4 cup

These are simple buns with candied citron, a hint of saffron, and a glaze of confectioners' sugar and egg white. Unassuming and delicious.

1. In a small saucepan, scald the milk by heating it just to the boiling point, and set aside to cool.

2. Fit the kneading blade firmly on the shaft in the bread pan. Carefully measure the flours, citron, sugar, dry milk, salt, and nutmeg, and transfer to the pan. Add the cooled milk, margarine, water, and yeast. Place the bread pan inside the machine and close the lid.

3. Program the breadmaker for the whole wheat dough mode. The unit will begin its operation.

4. At the end of the rising cycle, turn the dough out onto a lightly floured surface. With floured hands, pat into a 1/2-inch-thick square. With a sharp knife, cut the dough into squares. Lightly oil an 8-inch (or 9-inch) square baking pan and place the dough squares in the bottom. Cover and let the buns rise in a warm place for 30 minutes.

5. Bake the buns in a preheated 375°F oven for 20 to 25 minutes until golden. Meanwhile, in a small bowl, blend together the confectioners' sugar and beaten egg white(s). Remove the buns from the oven and brush with the glaze while still hot. Decorate the top with candied cherries and allow to cool. Serve barely warm. Makes 9 (or 12) buns.

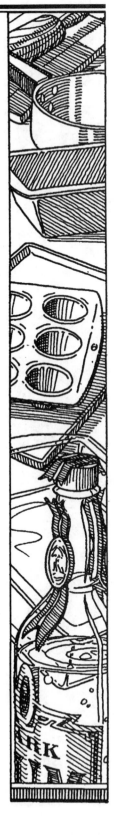

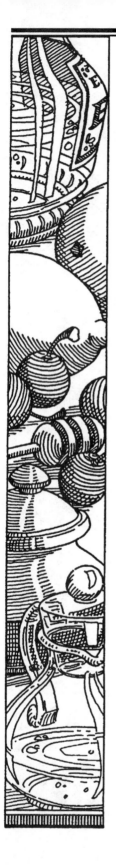

Finnish Easter Bread

INGREDIENT	1-POUND LOAF	1 1/2-POUND LOAF
Bread flour	1 3/4 cups	2 cups
Whole rye flour	3/4 cup	1 cup
Toasted and chopped almonds	1/2 cup	2/3 cup
Grated orange zest	1 tablespoon	1 1/2 tablespoons
Grated lemon zest	1 tablespoon	1 1/2 tablespoons
Crushed cardamom seeds	1 teaspoon	1 1/2 teaspoons
Sea salt	1 teaspoon	1 1/2 teaspoons
Date sugar	1 teaspoon	1 1/2 teaspoons
Water	1/2 cup	5/8 cup
Eggs, beaten	2 large	3 large
Canola, safflower, or sunflower oil	2 tablespoons	3 tablespoons
Brandy or cognac	3 tablespoons	1/4 cup
Active dry yeast	2 teaspoons	1 package
Dark raisins	1/2 cup	2/3 cup

You will really taste the cardamom, orange, and lemon in this delightful bread. Serve it with a spread of whipped cream cheese.

1. Fit the kneading blade firmly on the shaft in the bread pan. Carefully measure the dry ingredients and transfer to the pan. Add the water, eggs, oil, brandy, and yeast. Place the bread pan inside the machine and close the lid.

2. Program the breadmaker for the white bread mode. The unit will begin its operation.

3. At the end of the mixing cycle and just before the kneading cycle begins, add the raisins to the dough.

4. At the end of the baking cycle, remove the bread promptly from the machine, taking care, as the oven surfaces will be very hot. Invert the bread pan onto a wire rack and shake several times to dislodge the bread. Allow to cool for 30 minutes before slicing or wrapping for storage.

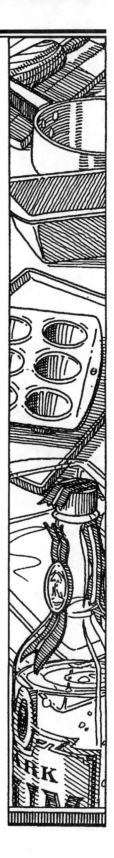

German Crescent Sweet Rolls

INGREDIENT	1-POUND LOAF	1¹/₂-POUND LOAF
Milk	1 cup	1¹/₄ cups
Whole wheat flour	1³/₄ cups	2 cups
Bread flour	³/₄ cup	1 cup
Dry milk	1 tablespoon	1 tablespoon
Sea salt	1 teaspoon	1¹/₂ teaspoons
Egg(s), beaten	1 large	2 large
Canola, safflower, or sunflower oil	1 tablespoon	2 tablespoons
Active dry yeast	1 package	4 teaspoons
Softened soy margarine	¹/₂ cup	²/₃ cup
Date sugar	²/₃ cup	³/₄ cup
Toasted and finely ground almonds	¹/₂ cup	³/₄ cup
Ground cinnamon	³/₄ teaspoon	1 teaspoon
Ground nutmeg	¹/₄ teaspoon	¹/₂ teaspoon
Egg yolk(s), beaten	1	2

*I have combined two very savory recipes
to create these light and buttery breakfast rolls
that are quite a treat.*

1. In a small saucepan, scald the milk by heating it just to the boiling point, and set aside to cool. Fit kneading blade firmly on shaft in the bread pan. Carefully measure the flours, dry milk, and sea salt, and transfer to the pan. Add cooled milk, egg(s), oil, and yeast. Place bread pan inside the machine and close the lid.

2. Program the breadmaker for the whole wheat dough mode. The unit will begin its operation. At the end of the rising cycle, turn the dough out onto a lightly floured surface. Cover and let rest for 10 minutes. Lightly oil a baking sheet. With a floured rolling pin, roll the dough out into a circle 10 inches (or 12 inches) in diameter. With a sharp knife, cut the circle into 10 (or 14) wedges.

3. Brush surface of dough with softened margarine. Reserving 2 tablespoons of date sugar, sprinkle each wedge with sugar, almonds, cinnamon, and nutmeg. Beginning at the wide end of each wedge, tightly roll up dough. Place rolls on prepared baking sheet 2 inches apart. Curl ends of each roll in toward middle to form slight crescent shape.

4. Cover the rolls loosely and set in a warm place to rise for 30 minutes. Brush the tops with egg yolk and sprinkle each with the remaining date sugar. Baked in a preheated 375°F oven for 15 to 20 minutes until golden. Transfer to a wire rack, ice with a glaze, if you like, and allow to cool for 15 minutes before serving. Makes 10 (or 14) crescents.

Italian Easter Bread

INGREDIENT	1-POUND LOAF	1½-POUND LOAF
Bread flour	2¼ cups	3 cups
Dry milk	1 tablespoon	1½ tablespoons
Sea salt	1 teaspoon	1½ teaspoons
White pepper	¼ teaspoon	½ teaspoon
Grated Asiago or Parmesan cheese	½ cup	¾ cup
Water	¾ cup	1 cup
Eggs, beaten	2 large	3 large
Olive oil	2 tablespoons	3 tablespoons
Active dry yeast	2 teaspoons	1 package

This bread, called "Cresca," is the traditional bread
served on Easter in parts of northern Italy.

1. Fit the kneading blade firmly
on the shaft in the bread pan. Carefully measure the dry
ingredients and transfer to the pan. Add the water, eggs,
1 tablespoon (or 2 tablespoons) of oil, and yeast. Place the bread
pan inside the machine and close the lid.

2. Program the breadmaker for
the white bread dough mode. The unit will begin its operation.

3. At the end of the rising cycle,
turn the dough out onto a lightly floured surface. Cover and let
rest 10 minutes. With floured hands, shape the dough into a
round loaf. Place the dough in a lightly oiled 8-inch (or 9-inch)
round cake pan. Cover loosely and let rise in a warm place for
30 minutes.

4. Brush the top of the dough
with 1 tablespoon olive oil and bake in a preheated 350°F oven
for 45 to 50 minutes, or until the loaf sounds hollow when
tapped. Transfer the bread to a wire rack and allow to cool
completely on the rack before slicing or wrapping for storage.

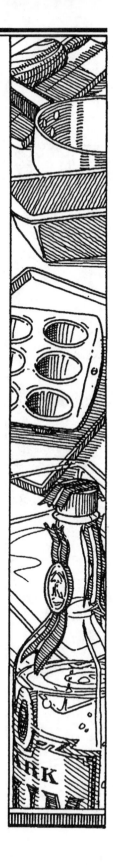

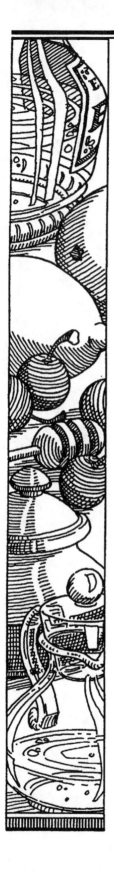

$\mathcal{K}$ulick

INGREDIENT	1-POUND LOAF	1$\frac{1}{2}$-POUND LOAF
Milk	$\frac{1}{4}$ cup	$\frac{1}{2}$ cup
Whole wheat flour	2 cups	2$\frac{1}{4}$ cups
Bread flour	$\frac{1}{2}$ cup	$\frac{3}{4}$ cup
Date sugar	3 tablespoons	$\frac{1}{4}$ cup
Grated lemon zest	1 teaspoon	2 teaspoons
Sea salt	$\frac{3}{4}$ teaspoon	1 teaspoon
Toasted and chopped almonds	$\frac{1}{4}$ cup	$\frac{1}{3}$ cup
Water	$\frac{1}{2}$ cup	$\frac{1}{4}$ cup plus 1 tablespoon
Egg(s), beaten	1 large	2 large
Dark rum	2 tablespoons	3 tablespoons
Canola, safflower, or sunflower oil	2 tablespoons	3 tablespoons
Active dry yeast	1 package	4 teaspoons
Chopped golden raisins	$\frac{1}{4}$ cup	$\frac{1}{3}$ cup
Chopped candied citron	$\frac{1}{4}$ cup	$\frac{1}{3}$ cup

This sweet holiday bread is a traditional Russian Easter bread that is filled with dried fruit and nuts.

1. In a small saucepan, scald the milk by heating it just to the boiling point and set aside to cool.

2. Fit the kneading blade firmly on the shaft in the bread pan. Carefully measure the flours, sugar, zest, salt, and almonds, and transfer to the pan. Add the cooled milk, water, egg, rum, oil, and yeast. Place the bread pan inside the machine and close the lid.

3. Program the breadmaker for the whole wheat mode. The unit will begin its operation.

4. At the end of the mixing cycle and just before the kneading cycle begins, add the raisins and citron to the dough.

5. At the end of the baking cycle, remove the bread promptly from the machine, taking care, as the oven surfaces will be very hot. Invert the bread pan onto a wire rack and shake several times to dislodge the bread. Top with one of the glazes in Chapter 10, and allow to cool completely on the rack before slicing or wrapping for storage.

Pineapple Streusel Buns

INGREDIENT	1-POUND LOAF	1½-POUND LOAF
Unsweetened pineapple slices in their own juice	1 can (5¼ ounces)	1½ cans
Bread flour	1¼ cups	1½ cups
Whole wheat flour	1 cup	1¼ cups
Bran cereal	¼ cup	¼ cup
Dry milk	1 tablespoon	1 tablespoon
Sea salt	1 teaspoon	1½ teaspoons
Ground allspice	½ teaspoon	¾ teaspoon
Water	⅓–½ cup	½–⅔ cup
Honey	2 tablespoons	3 tablespoons
Canola, safflower, or sunflower oil	1 tablespoon	2 tablespoons
Active dry yeast	1 package	4 teaspoons
Granola	1 cup	1⅓ cups
Date sugar	2 tablespoons	3 tablespoons

These moist, dense buns have a crunchy, sweet streusel topping and are always a hit with the kids.

1. Reserving the juice, drain pineapple and chop. Spread fruit onto a double thickness of paper towels and set aside to dry. Replace towels if they get too wet.

2. Fit the kneading blade firmly on the shaft in the bread pan. Carefully measure the flours, bran cereal, dry milk, sea salt, and allspice, and transfer to the pan. Measure the reserved pineapple juice and add enough water to measure $3/4$ cup (or 1 cup). Add this liquid to the bread pan along with the honey, oil, and yeast. Place the bread pan inside the machine and close the lid.

3. Program the breadmaker for the whole wheat dough mode. The unit will begin its operation. At the end of the mixing cycle and just before the kneading cycle begins, add the chopped pineapple to the dough.

4. At the end of the rising cycle, turn the dough out onto a lightly floured surface. Cover and let rest for 10 minutes. Lightly oil 6 (or 8) muffin cups. In a blender or food processor, chop the granola and sugar until medium-fine. With floured hands, divide dough into 6 (or 8) pieces and form each into a ball. Place one ball in each muffin cup. Sprinkle granola mixture (streusel) over the buns, pressing it lightly into the dough. Cover and set in a warm place to rise for 30 minutes.

5. Bake buns in preheated 400°F oven for 15 to 20 minutes until golden. Remove to a wire rack and cool for 10 minutes before serving. Makes 6 (or 8) buns.

Revolutionary Christmas Bread

INGREDIENT	1-POUND LOAF	1¹/₂-POUND LOAF
Whole wheat flour	2 cups	2¹/₄ cups
Bread flour	¹/₂ cup	³/₄ cup
Date sugar	2 tablespoons	3 tablespoons
Mashed potatoes	¹/₄ cup (about 1 small potato)	¹/₃ cup (about 1 small potato)
Sea salt	1 teaspoon	1¹/₂ teaspoons
Caraway seeds	1 teaspoon	1¹/₂ teaspoons
Ground allspice	¹/₂ teaspoon	³/₄ teaspoon
Ground mace	¹/₂ teaspoon	³/₄ teaspoon
Water	1 cup	1¹/₄ cups
Maple syrup	2 tablespoons	3 tablespoons
Canola, safflower, or sunflower oil	1 tablespoon	2 tablespoons
Active dry yeast	1 package	4 teaspoons
Dark raisins	¹/₄ cup	¹/₃ cup
Chopped candied citron	¹/₄ cup	¹/₃ cup

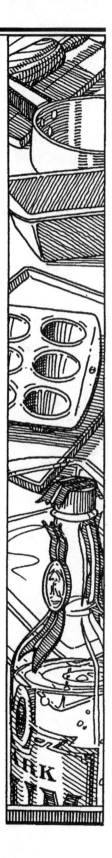

This bread brings us back to America's revolutionary period, during which it was one of New England's traditional holiday breads. It is filled with spices, candied fruit, and the delightful taste of maple syrup.

1. Fit the kneading blade firmly on the shaft in the bread pan. Carefully measure the dry ingredients and transfer to the pan. Add the water, maple syrup, oil, and yeast. Place the bread pan inside the machine and close the lid.

2. Program the breadmaker for the whole wheat mode. The unit will begin its operation.

3. At the end of the mixing cycle and just before the kneading cycle begins, add the raisins and citron to the dough.

4. At the end of the baking cycle, remove the bread promptly from the machine, taking care, as the oven surfaces will be very hot. Invert the bread pan onto a wire rack and shake several times to dislodge the bread. Allow to cool completely on the rack before slicing or wrapping for storage.

$\mathscr{S}$ticky Rolls

INGREDIENT	1-POUND LOAF	1¹/₂-POUND LOAF
Whole wheat flour	1¹/₂ cups	1³/₄ cups
Bread flour	1 cup	1¹/₄ cups
Sea salt	1 teaspoon	1¹/₂ teaspoons
Water	³/₄ cup	³/₄ cup plus 1 tablespoon
Canola, safflower, or sunflower oil	3 tablespoons	3 tablespoons
Maple syrup	2 tablespoons	3 tablespoons
Egg(s), beaten	1 large	2 large
Active dry yeast	1 package	4 teaspoons
Date sugar	1 cup	1¹/₃ cups
Softened soy margarine	1 cup	1¹/₃ cups
Vanilla extract	1 teaspoon	1¹/₂ teaspoons
Toasted and chopped pecans	1 cup	1¹/₃ cups
Ground cinnamon	1 teaspoon	1¹/₂ teaspoons
Ground nutmeg	¹/₂ teaspoon	1 teaspoon
Golden raisins	¹/₂ cup	³/₄ cup

These decadent rolls are made a wee bit healthier by using whole wheat flour as well as the bread flour. They are rich and tantalizing, making them perfect for special occasions.

1. Fit the kneading blade firmly on the shaft in the bread pan. Carefully measure the flours and salt and transfer to the pan. Add the water, oil, syrup, egg(s), and yeast. Place the bread pan inside the machine and close the lid.

2. Program the breadmaker for the whole wheat dough mode. The unit will begin its operation.

3. At the end of rising cycle, turn dough onto lightly floured surface. Cover and let rest for 10 minutes. Lightly oil 13x9x2-inch baking dish. In saucepan, melt $1/2$ cup of date sugar and $1/2$ cup of soy margarine. Bring mixture to boil and cook 1 minute. Remove from heat and stir in vanilla and $1/2$ cup of nuts. Immediately pour mixture into prepared dish.

4. With floured hands, pat dough into a $5/8$-inch-thick rectangle. Spread remainder of soy margarine over surface and sprinkle with remaining date sugar. Top with cinnamon, nutmeg, the remaining pecans, and raisins. Beginning at one of the long sides, roll dough up tightly, pinching the ends to seal. Using a sharp knife, cut into 1-inch slices. Arrange slices, cut side down, in the prepared dish. Cover loosely and set in a warm place to rise for 45 minutes or until doubled.

5. Bake the buns in a preheated 350°F oven for 40 to 45 minutes until golden. Cool in the pan for 5 minutes, then invert onto a serving plate. Allow the buns to cool slightly before serving. Makes 12 (or 16) buns.

$\mathcal{S}$tollen

INGREDIENT	1-POUND LOAF	1^1/$_2$-POUND LOAF
Milk	^{1}/$_2$ cup	^{2}/$_3$ cup
Bread flour	2^1/$_4$ cups	3 cups
Softened soy margarine	2 tablespoons	3 tablespoons
Dry milk	1 tablespoon	2 tablespoons
Sea salt	1 teaspoon	1^1/$_2$ teaspoons
Rum or brandy	3 tablespoons	^{1}/$_3$ cup
Eggs, beaten	2 large	3 large
Honey	1 tablespoon	1 tablespoon
Grated lemon zest	2 teaspoons	1 tablespoon
Active dry yeast	2 teaspoons	1 package
Toasted and chopped walnuts	^{2}/$_3$ cup	1 cup
Candied fruit	^{2}/$_3$ cup	1 cup
Golden raisins	^{2}/$_3$ cup	1 cup
Ground nutmeg	^{1}/$_4$ teaspoon	^{1}/$_2$ teaspoon
Ground mace	^{1}/$_4$ teaspoon	^{1}/$_2$ teaspoon
Melted soy margarine	^{1}/$_4$ cup	^{1}/$_4$ cup
Sifted confectioners' sugar	^{1}/$_4$ cup	^{1}/$_3$ cup

 *THE BREAD MACHINE GOURMET*

Top: Cinnamon Buns (page 246)
Bottom Left: Pineapple Streusel Buns (page 258)
Bottom Right: Shea's Apple Coffee Cake (page 200)

Top: *Sweet Potato Corn Muffins (page 240)
With Lemon, Honey, and Walnut
Cheese (page 279)
Bottom: Pumpkin Bread (page 236)*

A Christmas tradition at our house is making the German Christmas bread called Christollen. Even today, I eagerly await these wonderful loaves, which my father makes each holiday season. To me, Christmas is not Christmas without stollen.

1. In a small saucepan, scald the milk by heating it just to the boiling point, and set aside to cool.

2. Fit the kneading blade firmly on the shaft in the bread pan. Carefully measure the flour, dry milk, and salt, and transfer to the pan. Add the cooled milk, softened margarine, rum, eggs, honey, lemon zest, and yeast. Place the bread pan inside the machine and close the lid.

3. Program the breadmaker for the white bread dough mode. The unit will begin its operation.

4. At the end of the mixing cycle and just before the kneading cycle begins, add the nuts, candied fruit, raisins, and spices to the dough.

5. At the end of the rising cycle, turn the dough out onto a lightly floured surface. Cover and let rest for 10 minutes. Using floured hands, shape the dough into a thick oval. Lightly oil a large baking sheet and place the loaf in the center. Cover loosely and set in a warm place for 40 minutes.

6. Brush top lightly with melted margarine and bake in preheated 350°F oven for 60 to 70 minutes, or until loaf is golden brown. Transfer to wire rack and brush the surface with more melted margarine while bread is still hot. Heavily sprinkle the top with confectioners' sugar or top with one of the glazes in Chapter 10. Serve stollen thinly sliced.

*S*wedish Lussekatter

〜

INGREDIENT	1-POUND LOAF	1^1/$_2$-POUND LOAF
Bread flour	1 cup	1^1/$_4$ cups
Whole wheat flour	1 cup	1 cup
Toasted rolled oats	^{1}/$_2$ cup	^{3}/$_4$ cup
Crushed cardamom seeds	2 teaspoons	1 tablespoon
Sea salt	1 teaspoon	1^1/$_2$ teaspoons
Evaporated skim milk	^{7}/$_8$ cup	1 cup plus 2 tablespoons
Egg(s), beaten	1 large	2 large
Honey	2 tablespoons	3 tablespoons
Canola, safflower, or sunflower oil	1 tablespoon	1^1/$_2$ tablespoons
Active dry yeast	1 package	4 teaspoons
Heavy cream	3 tablespoons	^{1}/$_4$ cup
Date sugar	3 tablespoons	^{1}/$_4$ cup
Toasted and slivered almonds	^{1}/$_4$ cup	^{1}/$_3$ cup

December 13th is the official start of the Christmas season in Sweden, and this occasion is marked with the eating of these sweet buns.

1. Fit the kneading blade firmly on the shaft in the bread pan. Carefully measure the flours, oats, cardamom, and sea salt, and transfer to the pan. Add the milk, egg(s), honey, oil, and yeast. Place the bread pan inside the machine and close the lid.

2. Program the breadmaker for the whole wheat dough mode. The unit will begin its operation.

3. At the end of the rising cycle, turn the dough out onto a lightly floured surface. Cover and let rest for 10 minutes. Cut the dough into 8 (or 10) pieces. With floured hands, roll each piece into an 8-inch-long rope. Take the end of one of the ropes and place it on a lightly oiled baking sheet. Coil the dough, forming a round bun.

4. Lightly cover the buns and set in a warm place for 30 minutes. Brush each with cream and sprinkle with date sugar and almonds. Bake the buns in a preheated 350°F oven for 15 to 20 minutes until golden. Transfer to a wire rack and allow to cool slightly before serving warm. Makes 8 (or 10) buns.

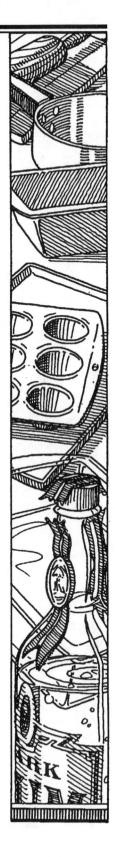

Toasted Almond Danish

INGREDIENT	1-POUND LOAF	1¹/₂-POUND LOAF
Milk	¹/₂ cup	³/₄ cup
Bread flour	2 cups	2¹/₄ cups
Whole wheat flour	¹/₂ cup	³/₄ cup
Dry milk	1 tablespoon	2 tablespoons
Sea salt	1 teaspoon	1¹/₂ teaspoons
Water	¹/₂ cup	¹/₂ cup
Canola, safflower, or sunflower oil	1 tablespoon	2 tablespoons
Honey	¹/₃ cup plus 1 tablespoon	¹/₂ cup
Active dry yeast	1 package	4 teaspoons
Melted soy margarine	6 tablespoons	¹/₂ cup
Toasted rolled oats	1 cup	1¹/₃ cups
Toasted and chopped almonds	¹/₃ cup	¹/₂ cup
Toasted and ground almonds	¹/₃ cup	¹/₂ cup

Almond pastries and large mugs of hot chocolate topped with fluffy mounds of whipped cream remind me of Sunday mornings when I was young.

INGREDIENT	1-POUND LOAF	1¹/2-POUND LOAF
Dried apricots, minced	6	8
Egg, beaten	1 large	1 large
Almond extract	1 teaspoon	1¹/2 teaspoons

1. In a small saucepan, scald the milk by heating it just to the boiling point, and set aside to cool.

2. Fit the kneading blade firmly on the shaft in the bread pan. Carefully measure the flours, dry milk, and sea salt, and transfer to the pan. Add the cooled milk, water, oil, 1 tablespoon (or 2 tablespoons) honey, and yeast. Place the bread pan inside the machine and close the lid.

3. Program the breadmaker for the white bread dough mode. The unit will begin its operation.

4. At the end of the rising cycle, turn the dough out onto a lightly floured surface. Cover and let rest 10 minutes.

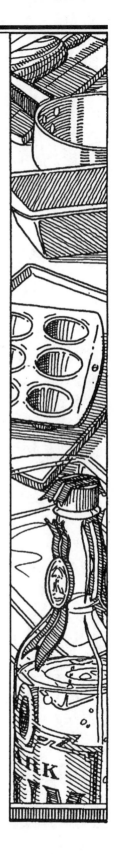

5. Lightly coat a large baking sheet with oil. In a small bowl, combine the melted margarine, oats, nuts, and apricots. With a wooden spoon, stir in the egg, the remainder of the honey, and the almond extract. Combine well.

6. Place the dough in the center of the baking sheet. With a floured rolling pin, roll the dough into a ¹/₂-inch-thick rectangle. Spread the oat mixture down the middle of the dough, leaving a 3-inch-wide strip on each side. On each side of the filling, cut 3-inch diagonal slits 2 inches apart. Fold alternating strips of dough over the filling to form a braid pattern. Pinch the ends of the strips to seal. Cover loosely and let rise in a warm place for 30 minutes.

7. Bake the Danish in a preheated 350°F oven for 25 to 30 minutes until golden. If desired, glaze the top while the Danish is still warm. Makes 8 (or 12) servings.

CHAPTER 10

WHIPS, DIPS, SPREADS, & GLAZES

Though often a popular choice, butter is not the only option for spreading on bread. There are many alternatives. Good bread gives you a wonderful opportunity to let your imagination soar. Topping or spreading your home-baked bread with one of the whips, dips, spreads, or glazes from this chapter can provide an exciting taste sensation.

Sometimes, instead of a spread, a simple wedge of cheese is the perfect adornment for your hot, fresh bread. Good cheeses offer a special aroma and flavor, while providing a bit of protein, too. My list of perfect bread cheeses includes Bel Paese, Boursin and other *triple-crèmes*, Brie, Camembert, Cheddar, Cheshire, Colby, Emmenthaler, Fontina, Gorgonzola, Havarti, Jarlsberg, Marscarpone, Muenster, Pont L'Eveque, Port Salut, Roquefort, Swiss, feta, farmer, and chèvre. Each of these cheeses is described at length in the Glossary of Ingredients, beginning on page 12.

Chutney Cheese

∽

Yield: 1¹/₂ cups   **Time: 10 minutes**

I have used both a good chutney and an orange marmalade as the main ingredient in this savory spread, and have found fantastic results with both.

INGREDIENT	AMOUNT
Softened cream cheese	8 ounces
Chutney or orange marmalade	¹/₂ cup
Plain nonfat yogurt	2 tablespoons
Apple cider vinegar	1 tablespoon
Curry	1 teaspoon
Ground ginger	¹/₂ teaspoon

1. In a small bowl, blend all the ingredients together with a wooden spoon until well combined.

2. Transfer the mixture to a container with a tight-fitting lid and store in the refrigerator until needed. This spread will keep for up to 10 days in the refrigerator.

Gorgonzola Cream

Yield: 1²/3 cups   **Time: 10 minutes**

*The unmistakable flavor of aged Gorgonzola
raises this simple spread to wonderful heights.*

INGREDIENT	AMOUNT
Yogurt Cheese (see page 282)	1 cup
Softened Gorgonzola cheese	³/4 cup
Olive oil	2 tablespoons

1. In a small bowl, beat together
the Yogurt Cheese, Gorgonzola, and olive oil until well blended.
Stir in the salt and pepper.

2. Transfer to a container with a
tight-fitting lid and refrigerate until needed.

3. Remove from the refrigerator
15 minutes before serving to allow the spread to soften slightly.
This spread will keep for up to a week in the refrigerator.

Garden Cheese

Yield: 1²/₃ cups   *Time: 15 minutes*

INGREDIENT	AMOUNT
Softened farmer cheese	12 ounces
Plain nonfat yogurt	2 tablespoons
Crushed garlic	1 clove
Sea salt	¹/₂ teaspoon
White pepper	¹/₄ teaspoon
Scraped and minced carrot	¹/₄ cup
Scrubbed and minced zucchini	¹/₄ cup
Shallot or scallion, minced	1

This light, fluffy cheese is filled with fresh vegetables and makes a wonderful spread for dark and rye breads.

1. In a medium bowl, beat the farmer cheese, yogurt, garlic, salt, and pepper together with a wooden spoon until well blended.

2. Add the carrot, zucchini, and shallot, and mix well. Transfer to a container with a tight-fitting lid and refrigerate until needed.

3. Remove from the refrigerator 15 minutes before serving. This spread will keep for up to a week in the refrigerator.

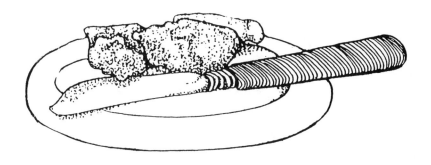

Greek Cheese

Yield: 2 cups   *Time: 10 minutes*

INGREDIENT	AMOUNT
Softened cream cheese or farmer cheese	12 ounces
Crumbled imported feta cheese	3/4 cup
Plain nonfat yogurt	2 tablespoons
Snipped fresh chives	2 tablespoons
Crushed garlic	1 clove
White pepper	1/2 teaspoon

Using imported feta cheese makes a great difference in the flavor of this spread. Domestic feta does not come close to the full-bodied taste of the Greek variety.

1. In a medium bowl, beat together the cheeses and yogurt until well blended. Stir in the chives, garlic, and white pepper.

2. Transfer to a container with a tight-fitting lid and refrigerate until needed.

3. Remove from the refrigerator 15 minutes before serving. This spread will keep for up to a week in the refrigerator.

Carrot Cheese

Yield: 2¹/₂ cups   *Time: 10 minutes*

Try this creamy spread with seed, nut,
or vegetable breads.

INGREDIENT	AMOUNT
Lowfat cottage cheese	8 ounces
Softened cream cheese	3 ounces
Scraped and finely minced carrot	¹/₄ cup
Crushed garlic	1 clove
Sea salt	1 teaspoon
White pepper	¹/₂ teaspoon

1. In a medium bowl and using a wooden spoon, beat together the cottage and cream cheeses until well blended. Stir in the rest of the ingredients

2. Transfer to a container with a tight-fitting lid and refrigerate until needed. This spread will keep for up to 1 week in the refrigerator.

Lemon, Honey, and Walnut Cheese

Yield: 2 cups

Time: 5 minutes to prepare; 1 hour to chill

This unusual combination creates a sweet and endearing cheese that is perfect to spread on freshly baked breads.

INGREDIENT	AMOUNT
Lowfat cottage cheese	16 ounces
Honey	$1/3$ cup
Fresh lemon juice	2 tablespoons
Grated lemon zest	1 tablespoon
Ground cloves	$1/4$ teaspoon
Toasted and finely chopped walnuts	$1/2$ cup

1. In a medium bowl and using a wire whisk, beat together the cottage cheese, honey, lemon juice, zest, and cloves. Stir in the walnuts.

2. Transfer to a container with a tight-fitting lid. Chill at least 1 hour before serving. This cheese will keep for up to a week in the refrigerator.

$\mathscr{A}$vocado Cheese

Yield: 2 cups

Time: 10 minutes to prepare; 1 hour to chill

INGREDIENT	AMOUNT
Ripe avocado, peeled, pitted, and cut into chunks	1 large
Lowfat cottage cheese	8 ounces
Softened cream cheese	8 ounces
Lime juice	1 tablespoon
Minced fresh cilantro or parsley	1 tablespoon
Sea salt	1/2 teaspoon
Ground cumin	1/4 teaspoon
White pepper	1/4 teaspoon

Be sure to use a ripe avocado with enough flavor to be noticeable in this fluffy spread.

1. Place the ingredients in a blender or food processor and pulse until well combined but not puréed.

2. Transfer to a container with a tight-fitting lid and refrigerate for at least 1 hour. This spread will keep for up to 3 days in the refrigerator.

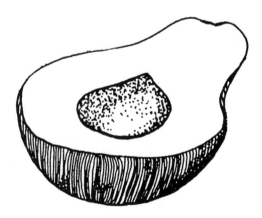

Caraway Spread

Yield: 1¼ cups

Time: 5 minutes

INGREDIENT	AMOUNT
Softened cream cheese	8 ounces
Half-and-half	¼ cup
Minced sweet yellow onion	1 tablespoon
Caraway seeds	2 teaspoons
Cayenne pepper	½ teaspoon, or to taste
Sea salt	½ teaspoon

If you wish, you can lighten this simple cheese by substituting a soft farmer cheese for the cream cheese.

1. In a small bowl, beat together the cream cheese and half-and-half until smooth. Stir in the onion, caraway seeds, cayenne pepper, and sea salt. Blend well.

2. Transfer to a container with a tight-fitting lid. Refrigerate until needed.

3. Remove the cheese from the refrigerator 15 minutes before serving. This spread will keep for up to a week in the refrigerator.

Yogurt Cheese

Yield: 1 cup   Time: 8 to 12 hours

*This is such a simple, healthy, and versatile cheese
that it can be eaten alone or used as a foundation
for many spreads.*

INGREDIENT	AMOUNT
Plain nonfat yogurt	16 ounces

1. Place the yogurt in a double thickness of cheesecloth and tie the corners together. Using a skewer or long-handled kitchen utensil, suspend this ball over a deep container, and refrigerate for 8 to 12 hours. (After 12 hours of draining, the cheese will have the consistency of cream cheese. If you prefer a softer version, drain for only 8 hours.)

2. Transfer the cheese to a container with a tight-fitting lid and use as needed. The cheese will keep for up to 2 weeks in the refrigerator.

Cottage Dip

∽

Yield: 2 cups   **Time: 10 minutes**

You will find this dip a delectable alternative to slathering your bread with butter.

INGREDIENT	AMOUNT
Lowfat cottage cheese	16 ounces
Plain nonfat yogurt	1/4 cup
Snipped fresh chives	1/4 cup
Crushed garlic	1 clove
White pepper	1/2 teaspoon
Sea salt	1/4 teaspoon

1. In a medium bowl and with a wire whisk, beat the ingredients together until well blended.

2. Transfer to a container with a tight-fitting lid and refrigerate until needed. This dip will keep for up to 5 days in the refrigerator.

Cucumber and Yogurt Dip

Yield: 2 cups   **Time: 15 minutes**

INGREDIENT	AMOUNT
Cucumber, peeled, halved lengthwise, and seeded	1 large
Sea salt	1 teaspoon
Plain nonfat yogurt	16 ounces
Fresh lemon juice	1 tablespoon
Crushed garlic	4 cloves
Minced fresh parsley	2 tablespoons
Minced fresh coriander, or dried coriander	1 teaspoon 1/4 teaspoon
Grated lemon zest	1 teaspoon
Ground cumin	1/2 teaspoon
Olive oil	2 tablespoons

THE BREAD MACHINE GOURMET

I particularly like this tangy, thick dip served with black breads such as pumpernickel.

1. Place the cucumber in a colander and sprinkle with salt. Allow to drain for 10 minutes, rinse, and pat dry. Finely chop the cucumber.

2. In a medium bowl, combine the yogurt, lemon juice, garlic, parsley, coriander, lemon zest, and cumin, and mix well. With a wire whisk, whip in the olive oil. Fold in the chopped cucumber.

3. Transfer to a tightly covered container and chill thoroughly before serving. This dip will keep for 3 days in the refrigerator.

Goat Cheese and Herbs

Yield: 1¹/₂ cups   *Time: 10 minutes*

INGREDIENT	AMOUNT
Softened farmer cheese	8 ounces
Soft chèvre cheese	¹/₂ cup
Crushed garlic	2 cloves
Olive oil	2 tablespoons
Minced fresh basil, or dried basil	1 tablespoon 1 teaspoon
Shallots, or scallions (including 1 inch of green tops), minced	4 3
Minced fresh parsley	1 tablespoon
Sea salt	¹/₂ teaspoon
Freshly ground black pepper	¹/₂ teaspoon

Be sure to use a soft, mild goat cheese for this very upscale spread that, while perfect with many of the breads in this book, also makes a dynamite spread for crackers.

1. In a small bowl, beat together the farmer cheese and chèvre until smooth. Stir in the garlic, oil, basil, shallots, parsley, salt, and pepper, and blend well.

2. Transfer to an attractive serving bowl and cover. Refrigerate until ready to use.

3. Remove the cheese from the refrigerator 15 minutes before serving. The cheese will keep for up to 4 days in the refrigerator.

*L*ight Herb Cheese

Yield: 1 cup   *Time: 10 minutes to prepare; 24 hours to chill*

INGREDIENT	AMOUNT
Yogurt Cheese (see page 282)	1 cup
Crushed garlic	2 cloves
Milk	2 tablespoons
Minced fresh parsley	1 tablespoon
Snipped fresh chives	2 teaspoons
Minced fresh basil	1 teaspoon
Fresh lemon juice	$1/2$ teaspoon

For prime flavor, use fresh herbs in this cheese spread
if at all possible.

1. In a small bowl and with a wooden spoon, beat all the ingredients together until fluffy.

2. Transfer to a container with a tight-fitting lid and refrigerate for 24 hours to allow the flavors to blend.

3. Remove from the refrigerator 15 minutes before serving. This cheese will keep for up to a week in the refrigerator.

Maple Cream

Yield: 1 cup   *Time: 5 minutes*

This light spread, a loaf of aromatic hot bread, and freshly brewed coffee or tea is a delightful way to start your day.

INGREDIENT	AMOUNT
Lowfat cottage cheese	4 ounces
Softened cream cheese	3 ounces
Maple syrup	1/4 cup
Milk	2 tablespoons
Ground cinnamon	1/2 teaspoon

1. In a small bowl, beat together the ingredients with an electric mixer until smooth.

2. Serve immediately, or refrigerate in a tightly covered container. This spread will keep for up to a week in the refrigerator.

$\mathcal{P}$eanut Butter Cheese

Yield: 1¹/₄ cups   **Time: 5 minutes**

*This is one of my favorite spreads, but then anything
made with peanut butter is usually a favorite of mine.*

INGREDIENT	AMOUNT
Part-skim ricotta cheese	8 ounces
Peanut butter	¹/₄ cup
Honey	2 tablespoons
Milk	2 tablespoons
Vanilla extract	2 teaspoons
Ground cinnamon	¹/₂ teaspoon
Ground nutmeg	¹/₄ teaspoon

1. In a blender or food
processor, blend all the ingredients together until smooth.

2. Transfer to a container with a
tight-fitting lid and refrigerate until needed. This spread will keep
for up to 10 days in the refrigerator.

Party Cheese

Yield: 1¹/₂ cups   *Time: 10 minutes*

INGREDIENT	AMOUNT
Softened ripe Camembert cheese	¹/₂ cup
Softened farmer cheese	4 ounces
Lowfat cottage cheese	4 ounces
Plain nonfat yogurt	¹/₃ cup
Milk	2 tablespoons
Dry mustard	1 teaspoon
Sea salt	¹/₂ teaspoon
Freshly ground black pepper	¹/₄ teaspoon

A good French Camembert cheese has a flavor that is difficult to describe, but one that infuses this spread with a mellow vitality.

1. With a sharp knife, carefully remove and discard the rind from the Camembert.

2. In a food processor or blender, blend all the ingredients until smooth.

3. Transfer to a container with a tight-fitting lid and refrigerate until needed.

4. Remove from the refrigerator 15 minutes before serving. This cheese will keep for up to a week in the refrigerator.

Pecan–Blue Cheese Spread

Yield: 1 1/2 cups *Time: 10 minutes*

INGREDIENT	AMOUNT
Softened cream cheese	8 ounces
Softened Roquefort or other blue cheese	1/2 cup
Brandy or cognac	1 tablespoon
Crushed garlic	1 clove
Sweet Hungarian paprika	1 teaspoon
Crushed dried hot red chilies	1/2 teaspoon, or to taste
Toasted and chopped pecans	1/2 cup

Any good blue cheese is appropriate to use in this tangy spread, although my favorite is a good Roquefort, which seems to add an air of sophistication as well as flavor.

1. In a small bowl, beat together the cream cheese and blue cheese until well blended. Stir in the rest of the ingredients.

2. Transfer to a container with a tight-fitting lid and refrigerate until needed.

3. Remove the cheese from the refrigerator 15 minutes before serving. It will keep for up to a week in the refrigerator.

$\mathcal{S}$esame Cheese

Yield: 2 cups   *Time: 5 minutes*

INGREDIENT	AMOUNT
Softened farmer cheese	16 ounces
Vermouth or dry white wine	6 tablespoons
Fresh lemon juice	4 teaspoons
Crushed garlic	1 clove
Tahini	1 teaspoon
Toasted sesame seeds	3 tablespoons
Sea salt	1/2 teaspoon
Freshly ground black pepper	1/4 teaspoon

This cheese has a very distinct flavor, so it is best served with breads that have a simple, uncomplicated taste.

1. In a medium bowl, beat together the farmer cheese, vermouth, lemon juice, garlic, and tahini until smooth.

2. Add the sesame seeds, salt, and pepper, and blend well.

3. Transfer to a container with a tight-fitting lid and refrigerate until needed.

4. Remove from the refrigerator 15 minutes before serving. This spread will keep for up to a week in the refrigerator.

Citrus Glaze

Yield: 1 cup   Time: 5 minutes

Sweet and tangy, I like this spread with Citrus Bread (page 166). For special occasions, try decorating the glaze with small pieces of candied citron.

INGREDIENT	AMOUNT
Sifted confectioners' sugar	1 cup
Softened soy margarine	2 tablespoons
Grated lemon zest	$1/2$ teaspoon
Grated orange zest	$1/2$ teaspoon
Fresh lemon juice	1 teaspoon
Fresh orange juice	1–2 tablespoons

1. In a small bowl, blend the confectioners' sugar, margarine, lemon zest, and orange zest together until well combined.

2. Add the lemon juice and enough orange juice to make a glaze of spreading consistency.

*H*oney Glaze

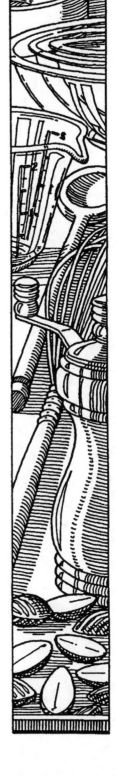

Yield: 1 cup   **Time: 5 minutes**

Chopped nuts can be sprinkled on top of this glaze, which is ideal for some of the nut breads found in Chapter 6, as well as some of the sweet egg and milk breads in Chapter 5.

INGREDIENT	AMOUNT
Sifted confectioners' sugar	3/4 cup
Softened soy margarine	1/4 cup
Egg white, beaten until frothy	1
Honey	3 tablespoons

1. In a small bowl, blend the confectioners' sugar and margarine together until well combined.

2. Stir the egg white and honey into the sugar-margarine mixture, and blend well.

Orange Nut Glaze

Yield: 1 cup   *Time: 5 minutes*

This glaze can be used on almost all fruit and nut breads but is something special on my Orange Raisin Bread (page 184).

INGREDIENT	AMOUNT
Sifted confectioners' sugar	1 cup
Softened soy margarine	2 teaspoons
Toasted and finely chopped walnuts	1/2 cup
Fresh orange juice	2–4 tablespoons

1. In a small bowl, blend together the sugar and margarine until well combined.

2. Add the nuts and stir in enough orange juice to make a spreadable glaze.

weet Rum Glaze

Yield: 1 cup   **Time: 5 minutes**

Very versatile, this glaze adds sweetness and just a hint of flavor to bread.

INGREDIENT	AMOUNT
Sifted confectioners' sugar	1 cup
Softened soy margarine	1 tablespoon
Dark rum	1^1/$_2$ tablespoons
Vanilla extract	^{1}/$_2$ teaspoon

1. In a small bowl, blend together the confectioners' sugar and margarine.

2. Stir the rum and vanilla extract into the sugar-margarine mixture, and blend well.

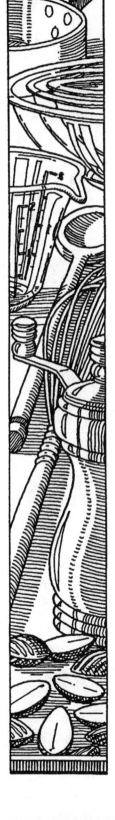

Chocolate Glaze

Yield: 1 cup   **Time: 15 minutes**

This absolutely scrumptious topping is perfect if you want to dress up a chocolate loaf for company.

INGREDIENT	AMOUNT
Semisweet chocolate chips	1/2 cup
Water	1/4 cup
Sifted confectioners' sugar	1 cup
Softened soy margarine	2 tablespoons
Vanilla	1/2 teaspoon
Dark rum	1–2 tablespoons

1. In a small saucepan over very low heat, melt the chocolate with the water, stirring constantly. Allow to cool for 5 minutes.

2. In a small bowl, combine the confectioners' sugar and margarine, and blend well.

3. Stir in the cooled chocolate, vanilla, and enough rum to make a spreadable glaze.

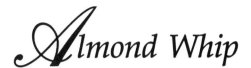lmond Whip

Yield: 2¹/₄ cups *Time: 10 minutes*

You will find this fluffy spread a wonderful addition to many of the nut or fruit breads found in this book.

INGREDIENT	AMOUNT
Lowfat cottage cheese	16 ounces
Softened cream cheese	3 ounces
Honey	¹/₄ cup
Almond extract	¹/₂ teaspoon

1. In a blender or food processor, whip all the ingredients together until smooth.

2. Transfer to a container with a tight-fitting lid and refrigerate until needed. This spread will keep for up to a week in the refrigerator.

INDEX

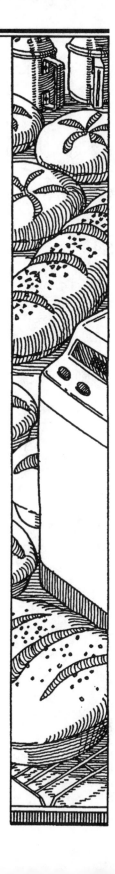

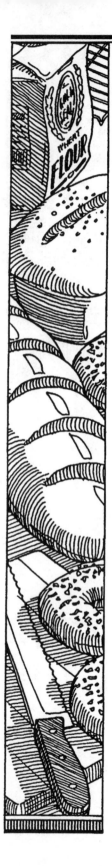

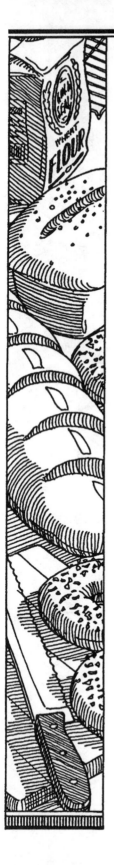